Henry Caner

A candid examination of Dr. Mayhew's Observations on the charter and conduct of the Society for the Propagation of the Gospel in Foreign Parts:

Interspers'd with a few brief reflections upon some other of the doctor's writings

Henry Caner

A candid examination of Dr. Mayhew's Observations on the charter and conduct of the Society for the Propagation of the Gospel in Foreign Parts:
Interspers'd with a few brief reflections upon some other of the doctor's writings

ISBN/EAN: 9783337713911

Printed in Europe, USA, Canada, Australia, Japan

Cover: Foto ©ninafisch / pixelio.de

More available books at **www.hansebooks.com**

A

CANDID EXAMINATION

O F

Dr. MAYHEW's Obfervations

ON THE

CHARTER AND CONDUCT

OF THE

SOCIETY for the propagation of the Gofpel
in foreign parts.

Interfpers'd with a few brief reflections upon fome other of the
DOCTOR's Writings.

To which is added,

A

LETTER to a FRIEND,

Containing a fhort Vindication of the faid SOCIETY
againft the Miftakes and Mifreprefentations of the Doctor in his
Obfervations on the Conduct of that Society.

By one of its Members.

Where envying and ftrife is, there is confufion and every evil work.
Out of the fame mouth proceedeth blefling and curfing. My
brethren, thefe things ought not fo to be.   James iii. 16. 10.

BOSTON, NEW-ENGLAND:

Printed and Sold by THOMAS and JOHN FLEET, in Cornhill; and
GREEN & RUSSELL, and EDES & GILL, in Queenftreet, 1763.

The CONTENTS.

Som---

A Candid Examination of Dr. MAYHEW'S Observations on the Charter and Conduct of the Society for the Propagation of the Gospel in Foreign Parts, &c.

IT is a long time since Dr. MAYHEW published his *modest* observations, on the charter and conduct of the Society for the propagation of the Gospel in foreign parts; and as no person hitherto has thought it worth his while to enter into a special examination of his principal argument, he probably concluded that his performance would not have met with a full reply. And in truth if he had drawn this conclusion from the nature and manner of his writing, as being too intemperately manag'd to deserve the notice of either a Gentleman or a Scholar, he had thought as other men do; for this, it has been said is the true reason, why he has been suffer'd to triumph thus long in his performance, and to boast of it as unanswerable. Every gentleman who has had a liberal and polite education, thinks it beneath his character to enter the lists with one who observes no measures of decency or good manners, nay who does not scruple to sacrifice the meek and gentle spirit of the Gospel to the gratification of a licentious and ungovern'd temper. Nor does the author of the present remarks pretend to rival him in this unbecoming talent; herein he is al-

B   low'd

low'd to reign without a competitor. But since he is liable to " think more highly of himself than he ought to think," and is already unhappily " wiser in his own conceit," than in any ones else; it may be esteem'd an act of charity to give him juster notions both of himself, and of his writings in general, but especially of his late performance, than he seems to have entertain'd.

THE method which will be used in discharging this charitable office, will be to represent the Doctor sometimes in the meek and benevolent light in which he affects to be considered; at other times, and by way of contrast to this, he will be produced in the light in which he has really exhibited himself: For altho' these are toto cœlo different, yet without a just and impartial representation of him in both these respects, it will be impossible to give him a true knowledge of himself, which is a point the author is very solicitous of; and is not without reasonable hopes of accomplishing.

To this purpose the author proposes to consult the Doctor's writings in general, which, as they are sufficiently voluminous, will afford abundant matter for such a representation, and being all of them corrected with his own hand, and sent abroad by his own appointment, may fairly be conceived to be a genuine picture of the man.

IT will be proper to begin with his last and highly boasted piece, entitled *Observations on the charter and conduct of the Society*, &c. The Introduction to which begins with these remarkable words, " There are some men who write—controversy " merely from a wrangling disposition, without any " regard to truth, right, or the importance of the " matters contested." Now one may defy any

man

man who fhall read this paffage, and efpecially if he
has read two or three volumes of fermons publifhed
in Bofton fince the year 1754, and fome occafional
thankfgiving difcourfes, in almoft every one of which
matters of controverfy have been dragg'd in, tho'
for the moft part as it were by head and fhoulders;
I fay, I defy any fuch man, not to think of one
who ftiles himfelf *paflor of the weft church in
Bofton.* And no doubt every one will be ready to
join with the Dr. in the words immediately following,
" that this is a turn of mind unbecoming a chriftian.''
And had he not been too unhappily inattentive to
his own maxim as before cited, doubtlefs he would
here have dropp'd his pen. " But fome of his
" friends" too " partial" indeed " in his favor" inju-
dicioufly prevented him from profiting by his own
admonition, having it feems " expreffed a defire that"
notwithftanding " *his*" great " *averfion to controverfy*
" —he would—communicate *fome* of his thoughts
" to the public, on the point in queftion." †

In the 8th page of his obfervations, the Doctor
affects to be very candid and ingenuous. " He is
" fenfible" he fays, " that the Society are a very re-
" fpectable Body, and to be treated with all the
" regard that is confiftent with truth and juftice—
" he declares it is by no means his intention to
" charge that venerable Body with any *wilful* known
" mifcondu&ct, or improper application of monies."
This is very commendable, if he had but kept it in
mind through the whole of his polite inquiry ; but
as though he was fenfible he fhould very foon break
through the aforefaid equitable rule, " he requefts
" the candor of his readers, that no advantage may
" be taken of any *incautious expreffion* that may
" *efcape* him in the purfuit of his argument, even
" tho'

† Obfervations p. 7.

(4)

" tho' it fhould at *firft* view, have the *appearanee* of
" fuch an accufation." ‡   This however is a reafonable poftulatum, and therefore it is not propofed,
nay, the author hereby promifes the gentleman that
he will not take advantage of *one* or even of *two*
incautious expreffions, that appear undefignedly to
have efcaped him, if at *firft view only* they have the
bare appearance of fuch an accufation ; but then he
cannot extend the fame indulgence to *very many*
expreffions importing a charge of wilful known mifconduct, and improper application of monies ;
efpecially, if not only at the *firft view*, but on a
fecond and third view, they do not appear to have
merely efcaped him, but were manifeftly intended
to fupport fuch an accufation.   Much lefs will he
be intitled to this indulgence, if it fhall appear that
the Society are directly charged by him with mifapplication of the monies committed to their truft, in
numerous paffages of his book, but moreover, that
the general defign of it was, an attempt to prove
this very point.

· THE Dr.'s book is entitled " Obfervations on the
"-charter and conduct of the Society, &c. *defigned*
" to fhew their non-conformity to each other."   In
fupport of this title, after fometimes contracting,
then ftretching and wire-drawing the fenfe of the
charter, feal, &c. of the Society, he concludes that
the *fole* defign of their inftitution was to propagate
the gofpel among the heathen, or in thofe colonies
whofe religious ftate was, and according to him, now
is, little better than heathenifm.   But this which he
afferts to be the laudable and only defign of their
inftitution, they have, he fays, grofsly perverted and
abufed.

                                                        THUS

‡ Obfervations P. 8.

THUS in page 55, he fays " the Society have ma-
" nifefted a fufficient forwardnefs to encourage and
" increafe fmall difaffected parties in our towns,
" upon an application to them." And in the 57th
page he reprefents the Society as hoping that thefe
fmall parties will by their influence gradually bring
on a general fubmiffion to an epifcopal fovereign ; and
" affirms that this has long been the formal defign
" of the Society, and is the true plan and grand
" myftery of their operations in New-England."

IN his 106th page he tells us that the " affair of
" Bifhops in America, has been a favourite object
" with the Society," and in the next page, that
" the Society fpare neither endeavours, applications,
" nor expence, in order to effect their *grand defign*
" of *epifcopizing* all New-England," and a few lines
further, " The Society have long had a *formal defign*
" to diffolve and root out all our New-England
" churches.—This (he fays) fully and clearly ac-
" counts for their being fo ready to encourage fmall
" epifcopal parties all over New-England, by fend-
" ing them miffionaries." In page 110 he affirms
that " the Society have been expending large fums
" every year in New-England, *quite beyond the defign*
" *of their inftitution*, to fupport and increafe the epif-
" copal party as fuch." In the fame page he charges
the Society with robbing the heathen to eafe and
gratify the epifcopalians here, and forms this conclufion upon his foregoing reprefentations, that " the
" Society are guilty of a flagrant abufe of a noble
" inftitution." And in the 112th page, that they
have " alienated their revenues from a truly noble
" to a comparatively mean, narrow, party defign."
After thefe feveral direct and plain accufations of the
Society as abufing their truft, and mifapplying the
money

money put into their hands, he wipes his mouth again, and abfurdly enough affures his reader, that " he wonld by no means be underftood as charging " fo refpectable a Body with any wilful criminal " abufe of power, or mifapplication of monies." i. e. he would not have the reader believe him ; for that is the fenfe of his words, as they ftand connected with what went before, if indeed they have any fenfe at all in them.

WILL he now have the *firmnefs* to affert, that all the *expreffions* and paffages which have been here quoted (and five times as many more might have been added) are only *incautious expreffions*, that inadvertently *efcaped him*, that they are not de-figned as matter of *accufation*, and that if poffibly they have fuch an *appearance*, it is only *at firft view?* If he fhould affert this, I am perfuaded his friends at leaft muft blufh for him. · Is the fupporting fmall parties in New-England, in order to facilitate the affair of *epifcopizing* the colonies, *the formal defign* of the Society, to which they give their chief atten-tion, and to which the largeft part of their fund is applied? Can he affert all this, and yet fay that he does not charge that venerable Body " with any " wilful known mifconduct, or improper application " of monies"?

PERHAPS this *confiftent* reafoner will chufe to fay that the Society are mifled, and form their plan upon the mifreprefentations of their *wicked* miffio-naries. Something like this is afferted in a note upon a thanfgiving fermon on the reduction of Canada, preached and publifhed by him in the year 1760. " It is probable that they [the Society] have " been grofsly impofed upon by falfe reprefentations " of the ftate of religion in thefe parts, which has

" been

" been the occasion of their employing so much of
" their charitable care about thofe who fo little need-
" ed it, to the neglect of thofe who were perifhing
" for want of it: For which impofitions, abufes and
" mifapplications, their deceivers are anfwerable ; if
" not to them, yet certainly to an HIGHER AU-
" THORITY." But furely whatever reprefentations
thefe miffionaries have made, the Society muft
judge whether the complying with fuch reprefentations was, or was not confiftent with their charter ;
fo that notwithftanding his ftriving to palliate his
accufation of the Society, by cafting the odium of
a pretended mifapplication of their charity on the
miffionaries, the flander will ftill remain where he at
firft placed it, on the Society themfelves. Befides, the
members of the Society are not all of them utterly
unacquainted with the plantations ; fome of them
have heretofore, and others do even now refide in
moft of the governments upon the continent, (New-
England not excepted) many of them not inconfi-
derable for their ftation, wifdom and integrity.
Thefe gentlemen muft therefore be alfo in a combi-
nation with the miffionaries to abufe the world, and
mifapply the monies entrufted with them. This feems
to be the confequence of his general accufation..

IF the Dr. would fay any thing further to
foften the odium of this accufation which he has
caft upon the Society, it muft be by afferting that
they did not underftand their own charter ; this, if
true, may ferve in fome meafure, to take off the
charge of wilful abufe and mifapplication ; and that
he fuppofes it true is clear from hence, that he has
fpent many pages and employed his great learning,
and penetration in explaining this intricate charter,
that the Society may no longer mifapply their charity

rity for want of underſtanding the real deſign of
their inſtitution. It may be queſtioned however,
whether his refin'd criticiſm and curious explanation
will merit the thanks of the venerable board. That
untoward word *orthodox*, which ſo much raiſes his
indignation wherever he meets with it, will not perhaps after all his learned pains, fairly comprehend
the diſſenters from a national eſtabliſhment. However that be, there is certainly no method of reconciling his candid profeſſions of juſtice, decency and
reſpect towards the Society, or his ſolemn declaration that it is not his intention to charge that
venerable Body with *wilful known* miſconduct : I
ſay, it is impoſſible to reconcile theſe things, with
the numerous abuſes, accuſations and indecencies
which have been already produced, and with which
he has treated that reſpectable Body directly or implicitly, in almoſt every page of his book.

- In ſhort, the Society either have, or have not
acted contrary to the meaning and deſign of their
charter ; that they have not, is at leaſt highly probable from the character of wiſdom, honor and
piety, which the world will generally allow to thoſe
of them at leaſt, who are chiefly active and intereſt-
ed in managing their affairs. If they have acted
contrary to the deſign of it, as the Dr. affirms (and
pretends to think he has prov'd) they have either
done ſo *wilfully*, or thro' ignorance. That they
have not done it wilfully, the Dr. himſelf allows ;
it remains then, according to him, that their miſconduct is owing to ignorance: Either they have
miſunderſtood the true and real deſign of their
charter, or have not a competent knowledge of the
ſtate of religion in the plantations, or how their
affairs are conducted there, being impoſed on by the
repreſentation

(9)

reprefentation of their miffionaries, or that both
thefe things concur to. miflead them, into an abufe
of their inftitution. The latter feems to be his fenfe
of the thing, viz. that they are ignorant both of the
true meaning of their charter, and alfo of the ftate.
of religion in the plantations ; fo: he fays in the
clofe of his introduction, that " the profefs'd defign of his obfervations is to fhew, that they (the
" Society) have in fome refpects counteracted and
'. defeated the truly noble ends of their INSTITU-
" TION, however *contrary to their intention*." Whether they have done fo or not, will fall under examination hereafter. In the mean time I fhall take
leave of his introduction with this fingle remark,
that from the paffages already quoted, as well as
from many others that might have been produced.
from this curious book of obfervations, it appears
that the profeffions of candor and ingenuity which
the Dr. fet out with, and his declaration of refpect
for fo venerable a body as the Society, are more
affectation and grimace, and tend only to prove that
he " knows not what manner of fpirit.he is of.",

It was obferved before, that according to the Dr's
reprefentation the Society are ignorant of the true
fenfe and meaning of their charter, and alfo of the.
ftate of religion in the plantations ; for he afferts
that they have greatly perverted the defign of their
inftitution, and yet will not allow their mifconduct.
to be wilful ; it remains therefore that their mifapplication of the truft they have undertaken, is owing
to ignorance.

It will be proper therefore to inquire firft, Whether
the Society muft not be fuppofed to have a competent
knowledge of the ftate of religion in the plantations,fo far at leaft as relates to the defign of their incorporation. And, B 2. Whether

2 Whether they may not alfo reafonably be fuppofed to underftand the true fenfe, meaning and defign of their charter ; for if thefe two things can
be proved to the fatisfaction of difinterefted and
unprejudiced people, it will follow, either that the
Society are not chargeable with mifcondu&t and mifapplication of their charity, or if they are fo, that
fuch mifcondu&t is known, wilful and intended,
which the Dr. does not allow.

The firft thing to be examined is, Whether the
Society have not a competent knowledge of the
ftate of religion in the plantations. Dr. Humphries
in his hiftory of the Society page 22d, acquaints us,
that " upon their firft engaging in this work the.
" Society prefently perceived it confifted of three
" great branches, the care and inftru&tion of our
" own people, fettled in the colonies ; the conver-
" fion of the Indian Savages, and the converfion
" of the Negroes. The Englifh planters had a
" title to their firft care" &c.—" The Society began
" therefore with the Englifh, and foon found there
" was more to be done among them, than they had
" as yet any views of effe&ting." He then proceeds
to give " a fmall fketch of the ftate and condition
" of each colony, formed from accounts, the Go-
" vernors, and perfons of the beft note, fent over
" to the corporation." I fhall omit what is faid of
the fouthern *heathenifh* colonies as Dr. Mayhew
modeftly calls them, becaufe thefe he allows to be
proper objects of the Society's charity, and proceed
to the ftate of religion in New-England as reprefented in the hiftory before mentioned. After fpeaking
of the firft fettlement of the country, and the ftate
of religion in the early days of it, Dr. Humphries
proceeds to fay,—" Since that time great numbers
" of

" of people, members of the church of England,
" have at-different times fettled there, who thought
" themfelves furely entituled, by the very New-
" England charter to a liberty of confcience in the
" worfhipping of God after their own way. Yet
" the Independents (it feems) were not of this fen-
" timent, but acted as an *eftablifhment*." " The
" members of the church of England in Bofton
" met with fo much obftruction in attempting to fet
" up that form of worfhip, that they were obliged
" to petition the King for protection. Their peti-
" tion was granted, and a Church thereupon erect-
" ed, which occafioned the members of the church
" of England in many other towns in New-England
" to declare their defire of the like advantage, and
" accordingly wrote very zealous letters to bifhop
" Compton, for minifters ; and now it appeared
" they were a very confiderable body of people."*
From thefe feveral paffages, it appears that the Society
did not proceed haftily and without due caution and
information of the ftate of religion in the colonies
which they propofed to affift. Dr. Humphries goes
on and fums up the religious ftate of the colonies
in a brief reprefentation of it, from the memorials
of Governor Dudley, Col. Morris, and Col. Heathcote. I fhall pafs over the fouthern colonies for
the reafon before mentioned, and come to New-
England.—" In Connecticut colony in New-England
" there are about 30000 fouls, of which when
" they have a minifter among them, about 150
" frequent the church, and there are 35 commu-
" nicants. In Rhode-Ifland and Narraganfet, which
" is one government, there are about 10000 fouls,
" of which about 150 frequent the church, and
" there are 30 communicants. In Bofton and Pif-

* Humph. Hift p. 39. " cataway

" cataway governments, there are about 80000
" fouls, of which about 600 frequent the church,
" and 120 the facrament."

After fuch particular information from the memorials of thefe honorable perfons, perhaps no man
except Dr. Mayhew and his voucher, will fuppofe
the Society could be ignorant of the ftate of religion
in this part of the world, nor confequently where
it was moft proper to employ their charity. Agree-
ably Dr. Humphreys acquaints us that " the Gover-
" nors of feveral colonies, and other Gentlemen of
" character abroad, and merchants here in London,
" having given fuch a particular defcription of the
" religious ftate of the plantations ; the Society
" found it was high time to enter upon the good
" work" * efpecially as " great numbers of the in-
" habitants of various humors, and different tenets
" in religion, began to contend with great zeal,
" which fhould be firft fupplied with minifters of
" the church of England, and wrote very earneft
" letters to theSociety—They (the Society) thought
" any further delay now would be inexcufable, after
" the people had preffed fo earneftly for their af-
" fiftance." Yet as if all this care was infufficient,
and that the Society might leave no method unat-
tempted, for gaining a more perfect knowlege of
the ftate of religion in the colonies, " before they
" proceeded to appoint miffionaries to particular
" places, (they) refolved to fend a travelling miffio-
" nary, who fhould travel over, and preach in the
" feveralGovernments,on the continent of theBritifh
" America." † Accordingly they did fend the Rev.
Mr. Keith, who landed at Bofton on the 11th of
June 1702. and in the courfe of two years travel'd
over

* Humph. Hift. p. 44, 45.   † Ditto 73,74.

over and preached in all the Governments betwixt
Pifcataway river and North-Carolina inclufively, when
having finifhed his miffion he returned to England,
and publifhed a full account of his labours. ‡ One
thing in his narrative I fhall juft mention, viz. That
" in divers parts of New-England, he found not
" only many people well affected to the Church,
" who had no church of England minifters, but
" alfo feveral New-England minifters defirous of
" epifcopal ordination, and ready to embrace the
" church worfhip, fome of whom both hofpi-
" tably entertained Mr. Keith and Mr. Talbot (who
" had joined Mr. Keith as an affiftant) in their
" houfes, and requefted them to preach in their
" congregations, which they did, and received great
" thanks, both from the minifters and from the
" people." *

" Mr. Keith in the conclufion of his narrative re-
" prefented to the Society, the want of a great num-
" ber of minifters for a people difperfed over fuch
" large countries," and among others makes mention
of Narraganfet, Swanfey, Little Compton & Rhode-
Ifland in New-England, which Places had engaged
him to prefent their humble requefts to the Society, to fend minifters among them.†

Yet notwithftanding this particular information,
fupported by many earneft petitions from the plantations for minifters of the church of England,
" the Society thro' the whole management of the
" truft, have been fo far from obtruding the church
" of England worfhip upon any fort of people
" abroad—that they have not been able to give any
" affiftance to great numbers of people, who have
" in very moving terms, with a true chriftian fpirit
" requefted

‡ Humph. Hift. p. 74.   * Ditto 78, 79.   † Ditto.

" requefted it ; and whom they *knew* to ftand very
" much in want of it. There remain upon
" their books numerous petitions of this fort."—
I fhall omit thofe from the fouthern colonies, for
the reafons before mentioned, and proceed to that
of New-England, which asDr.Humphreys acquaints
us (page 61) " tho' before provided with an inde-
" pendent and prefbyterian miniftry, yet had great
" numbers of inhabitants, who could not follow
" that perfuafion, but were exceeding defirous of
" worfhipping God, after the manner of the church
" of England. I fhall give the reader (fays he) a
" few petitions which fhew plainly the Society did
" not concern themfeives here, till they were loudly
" called upon ; and that the inhabitants in many
" places, did not only fend petitions for minifters,
" but alfo built churches before they had any mi-
" nifters, which is an uncontroulable evidence—
" that the people themfelves defired to have the
" church of England worfhip,with a hearty zeal and
" true fincerity." The Dr. then proceeds to fpecify
as petitioners feveral inhabitants of Rhode-Ifland,
Narraganfet,Newbury, Marblehead,New-Hampfhire,
Little Compton and Tiverton, Braintree near Bofton,
and Stratford in Connecticut.* " The cafe of thefe
" two laft towns he tells us was alfo further recom-
" mended to the Society's care, by gentlemen of
" confiderable figure and intereft. Colonel Morris
" preffed very earneftly for a minifter for Braintree,
" and Colonel Heathcote, for another, for the peo-
" ple of Connecticut colony ; great numbers of
" whom were very earneft to have a minifter of the
" church of England. Robert Hunter, Efq; Go-
" vernor of New-York, in the year 1711, writes
" thus

* Humph. Hift. p. 61, 62.

" thus to the Society, concerning the people at
" Stratford : When I was at Connecticut, thofe of
" our communion at the church at Stratford, came
" to me in a body ; and then, as they have fince
" by letter, begged my interceffion with the vene-
" rable Society, and the right reverend the Lord
" bifhop of London, for a miffionary ; they ap-
" peared very much in earneft, and are the beft fet
" of men I met with in that country."

How thefe feveral teftimonies which have been
produc'd will operate upon Dr. Mayhew, it is not
eafy to fay; but to the fober, judicious and unprejudiced, the following conclufions may perhaps be
thought fairly drawn, viz. That the Society have
omitted no proper means of information concerning the ftate of religion in the colonies—That their
religious ftate muft therefore be competently known
to that venerable board—And that if they have
been guilty of any notorious mifconduct or mifapplication of their charity, it could not be owing to
ignorance of the true condition of things abroad,
but muft be attributed to fome other caufe : For
allowing what the Dr. has moft uncharitably inti-
mated, that the miffionaries have mifreprefented the
condition of things among us, and by that means
endeavoured to miflead the Society to an improper
application of the monies lodged in their hands ;
yet can any modeft perfon fuppofe that Governors
of colonies, merchants, and other gentlemen of
character, have all along combined with the faid
wicked miffionaries, to abufe and miflead the Society
into a wrong difpofition of their charity ? Or is it
probable that their own members, feveral of whom
do refide in the colonies, fhould confpire with the
worthy perfons before mentioned to carry on the
deceit ?

deceit ? It is hoped the Dr. himſelf is not ſo far involved in a party ſpirit as to affirm the probability of this, if he is, without doubt he is alone in ſuch an uncharitable cenſure. And therefore this point may be left without any further remarks, to the public opinion.

The ſecond Inquiry is ; Whether the Society may not reaſonably be ſuppoſed to underſtand the true ſenſe, meaning and deſign of their Charter.

To thoſe who examine the liſt of members of which the Society is compoſed, as it is exhibited in the yearly abſtract of their proceedings, the preſent inquiry will appear very extraordinary. That a Sett of Gentlemen, many of them highly diſtinguiſh'd in the world for their great parts, and extenſive knowlege, ſhould miſtake, or be at a loſs about the true meaning of a charter, which has nothing at all in it that is intricate or obſcure, is what no reaſonable perſon will admit. And notwithſtanding the Dr's *refined criticiſm*, ſome may perhaps imagine that it muſt argue no ſmall meaſure of ſelf-ſufficiency in any perſon to oppoſe his ſingle ſentiment, to that of ſo learned and reſpectable a body. Few beſides the Dr. himſelf, will really believe that they needed his aſſiſtance for acquiring a right underſtanding of their charter. If we ſhould ſuppoſe, that thoſe very learned divines, who from the beginning have compoſed a conſiderable part of that body, ſhould be leſs acquainted with the phraſe and purport of an inſtrument in ſome meaſure foreign to their profeſſion ; yet doubtleſs the Lord Chancellor, the chief Juſtices of the King's Bench and common pleas, whoſe peculiar profeſſion it is, may be ſuppoſed to underſtand the nature of inſtruments of this kind. And as the Society are obliged to exhibit an annual account of their

their proceedings to thefe very learned and worthy perfons, it is furprizing that they fhould fuffer them to proceed above 60 years, without once acquainting them that their conduct was not agreeable to the *Letter and Spirit* of their charter. That the Society fhould at laft be obliged to a *profound critic* inNew-England for an ellucidation of this kind, after having fo many years ftood the teft of an annual examination, by thofe whom the royal wifdom thought proper to appoint as their fupervifors——Believe it they that can—

Some friend of the Dr's may poffibly here cry out, what would this remarker be at? The Dr. has plainly prov'd that the Society have been guilty of great mifconduct, have acted quite inconfiftent with the intent and defign of their charter, and from a principle of charity is willing to impute it to mifinformation, or ignorance; while this writer who affects to be the friend of the Society is labouring to defeat the Dr's benevolent purpofe, and feems as tho' he defigned to prove their mifconduct to be wilful.

After thanking the candid Dr. for his good intention, the author confeffes it is his opinion, and he thinks it has in fome meafure been prov'd; either that the Society have not acted inconfiftent with their charter, or if they have done fo, that it was knowingly, wilfully and defignedly done. The author thinks, as all reafonable men muft think, that the Society do very well underftand the defign and meaning of their charter—And alfo that they have a competent knowledge of the ftate of religion in the plantations.

If thefe two things are allowed, the conclufion will unavoidably be what was mentioned before, viz.

C   either

either that the Society have *wilfully* mifconducted, or elfe, that there has been no mifconduct in the cafe—That they have *wilfully* mifconducted the Dr. difallows, ther.fore, there has been no mifconduct at all.—Here then the argument and imputation which the Dr. has caft upon the Society, drop of courfe.

However, tho' the Dr. has been candid enough to clear the Society from any intentional abufe of their charter, poffibly others may not be fo ingenuous. Befides it may be efteemed unfair to take this advantage of the Dr's conceffion, to the neglect of thofe many curious arguments he has brought to prove what he had before given up ; for notwithftanding the inconfiftency of it, he has throughout his book laboured to prove ('that which he gave up in the beginning ;) that the Society have really been guilty of wilful and defigned abufe of their truft. And therefore the author hopes the Dr. will forgive it, if upon a general view of the obfervations, he is led to queftion the finceritv of that declaration before mentioned, viz. " That it is not his intention " to charge that venerable body (the Society) with " any wilful known mifconduct or improper appli- " cation of monies."

Mr. Noah Hobart (whom by the way the Dr. has dubb'd a *bifhop*, for his heroic exploits in this controverfy) has plainly fpoke out, and directly charged the Society with a defigned abufe and pervertion of their truft, at leaft fince the firft ten years after their incorporation,† though indeed like the Dr. he afterwards feems difpofed in fome meafure to retract the charge, and chufes rather to impute it to their ignorance of the ftate of religion in New-England, and

† Hobart's 2d Addrefs, p. 126. con pur'd with following pages.

and to the impofition and mifreprefentation of their
wicked millionaries. * But the author conceives it
has already been proved that their conduct cannot
be imputed to a want of knowledge, and whatever
the difpofition of Mr. Hobart or his copier may be,
it is prefumed that an accufation of the Society as
wilfully betraying their trult, will be received by the
impartial world, with the refentment it deferves. It
is not the Society alone, who are thus unjuftly ar-
raigned by thefe licentious pens, but the integrity
and honor of their infpectors alfo, the Lord chancellor and the chief juftices of the King's bench,
who yearly examine and approve their tranfactions,
do of confequence fuffer impeachment by their ca-
lumny; nay the extenfive abufe reaches to every
benefactor to that Society, who, as an annual account of their proceedings is publifhed and put into
their hands, muft be fuppofed to approve them, fince
otherwife it is more than probable they would have
withdrawn their affiftance.

As for the learned and ingenious Dr. Mayhew,
he certainly defended very low, when he vouchfafed
to become the tranfcriber of Mr. Hobart's addrefs,
for (excepting fome perfonal reflections upon his
antagonift) there appears little elfe throughout his
obfervations, befides a fervile copying of that curious
price of defamation. The method indeed he may
claim to himfelf, and fometimes the phrafe and manner of expreffion. The Dr. owns " the book has
been of fervice to him," and promifed to " make
proper acknowledgments wherever he fhould make
ufe of it" yet has not perhaps always been fo good
as his word; nor will the empty honor of a bifhop
which he arbitrarily confers on him, be allow'd a
                                                    fufficient

* Vid. Hob. 2d Addrefs, p. 145.

fufficient compenfation for the liberties of this kind which he has taken. He afferts that " Mr. Hobart wrote fo folidly, and judicioufly upon the fubject, that it was hardly needful for him to fay any thing," this is granted, unlefs he could have advanced fomething new, which the other had not offer'd before ; efpecially as Mr. Hobart's peice received as folid and judicious an anfwer, which the Dr. thought proper wholly to neglect. In truth, had the Dr. but carefully read the Rev. Mr. Beach's difpaffionate but mafterly reply to Mr. Hobart's fecond addrefs, he might have feen a full and compleat anfwer to all he has written (except what is merely perfonal) without breaking in upon that peaceable difpofition which gives him fuch " an *averfion to controverfy.*"

The Dr. affirms p. 18. That " nothing is to be
" fuppofed the object, or any part of the object of
" this charitable and royal inftitution, but what
" plainly appears to be really fo, from the very
" words of the charter"— and a little after " the
" words of the charter itfelf muft determine and
" limit the fenfe of the royal Granter, and confe
" quently the legal power conferred on the —
" Grantees." We fhall fee prefently how far the Dr. adheres to his own invariable rule of interpretation. He confeffes " that the Britifh plantations " or the King's fubjects were really the primary, " more immediate object of this inftitution." And pray why not the fole and entire object of it ? There is certainly no other object " particularly expreffed" in the charter, befides that of the King's fubjects. Has he forgot what he had afferted but a few lines before, that " nothing is to be fuppofed " any part of the object of this inftitution, but what " plainly appears to be fo from the very words of
" the

" the charter." Why then are the King's fubjeᵆs faid to be the *primary, more immediate,* and not the *fole* objeᵆ of their inftitution ? fince they are the only objeᵆ exprefly mentioned in the *very words of the charter.* It was a ftrange overfight in this great critic, to depart fo fuddenly from his invariable rule ; or perhaps there was a defign to be ferved in interpreting the charter by way of implication, tho' exprefly contrary to his own rule of a literal inter- pretation ; and that was to perfwade the world, that this fociety was erected chiefly for propagating the Gofpel among the Indians. To this purpofe he has conveniently contrived two objeᵆs of this inftitu- tion, the one " primary and immediate" " (the King's " fubjeᵆs") " the other the grand ultimate objeᵆ, " which is the Indians bordering on the colonies." But becaufe the exprefs words of the charter, which he had reprefented as the fole rule of their conduᵆ, unluckily make no mention of " this grand ulti- mate defign", therefore he found himfelf under a neceffity of departing from the rule himfelf had contrived, in order to adapt one of greater latitude. Indeed the Dr. affures us that this phrafe " *the pro- pagation of the gofpel in thofe parts,"* neceffarily " includes the grand ultimate defign" before men- tioned " of chriftianizing the Indians." But pray Dr. why fo ? Is not the defign of that phrafe *the propagation of the gofpel* fully anfwer'd, by preach- ing it to thofe of the King's fubjeᵆs who feem to be abandon'd to atheifm and infidelity, and to thofe other " inferior fubjeᵆs the flaves"? many of whom even in New England are yet in a ftate of Heathe- nifm. Does not the royal Grantor fay exprefly, " we think it our duty to promote the glory of God, by the inftruction of *our people* in the chriftian religion ?"

religion ?" Is there a single word about the heathen bordering on our colonies ? Why will he then force upon us a defign which the charter does not mention?

What is here faid is not intended to prove that the Society have not a power by their charter to propagate the Gofpel among the heathen, for they really have fuch a power, and have accordingly made ufe of it, whenever opportunity has offer'd to do it with fuccefs ; and will continue to do fo notwith-ftanding his endeavours to mifreprefent, and leffen the merit of their pious labours. But the author's intention is to fhow the Dr. the fophiftry of his argument, and that the rule he lays down for inter-preting the charter, would, if admitted, exclude the Society from this good work, and confequently that his argument by proving too much, proves nothing at all.

The truth is, the Society have by their charter, not only a legal power of propagating the Gofpel among fuch of the King's fubjects as are in danger of lofing their chriftianity thro' atheifm or infidelity, and among the heathen who have not fo much as heard of the name of Chrift : But (as miniftring greatly to thefe purpofes) of fupporting the means of religion among thofe who have already, or who incline to receive it according to the legal eftablifh-ment and provifion of the church of England. In fhort whatever legal means are found neceffary or conducive to fecure or propagate the profeffion of chriftian religion as it is eftablifhed in England, and all other his Majefty's dominions (Scotland excepted) and made a part of the conftitution of the Englifh *nation* ; the Society have a right by their charter to make ufe of, underftood in that generous view, ori-ginally defigned and intended by the Grantor.

But

But to this the Dr. further objects, that the Grantor " King William himself was bred up in " the calviniftic principles and difcipline, quite oppo- " fite in fome refpects to the epifcopal, and is gene- " rally fuppos'd to have retain'd a regard for the " principles of his education all along ; tho' as King " of England and head of that church, there was " a neceflity of his *externally conforming* to its rites " and difcipline"—The reader is defired to ftop here for a moment, and indulge his aftonifhment. Was this glorious deliverer then a finifh'd hypocrite ? Was he under a neceflity of acting contrary to his confcience? of conforming externally to the church of England while his heart was not in all this ? What blacker picture could he have drawn of thofe whom he calls " the infamous race of the Stewarts"* than he has here given of this excellent prince ? A Prince for whom he pretends a refpect, at leaft as much refpect as he is capable of paying to any crowned head : For he affures us in a very folemn manner, that " the greateft part of mankind now " are, and almoft always have been oppreffed by " wicked tyrants, called civil rulers, Kings and " Emperors".† So this perhaps is to pafs for a light cenfure upon the memory of our glorious de- liverer. And this fuppofitious reflection upon King William was introduced it feems to prove that he could not look upon the miniftry in the church of England as orthodox, in oppofition to thofe who diffent from the eftablifhment. But he might have found a better argument to prove that he could and did look upon it in that light ; for certainly better evidence could not be given of his regard for the church of England, and his defire to fee it take : place

* Vid. Than. Serm. 1758 p. 48. † Vid. Serm 12. p 426. Vol. I.

place and flourifh in New-England, than his giving
a hundred pounds fterling per annum out of the
privy purfe for fupporting a minifter of the church
of England in Bofton, and his beftowing a valuable
library of books on King's chapel in that town ;
to which (tho' not immediately relative to N. England) gratitude will oblige all true fons of the
church of England in America to add, his royal
foundation of a college at Williamfburg in Virginia
for the fame noble purpofe. If the King himfelf
could fo liberally part with his own money to fupport what the Dr. calls the *peculiarities of epifcopacy ;*
it can hardly be doubted but that he would readily
encourage the charity of others in doing the like.
So that it is not quite fo " unnatural" as the Dr. imagines " to fuppofe that *that* noble fpiritedPrince had
" fuch an intention." Indeed it would be unnatural
to fuppofe the contrary, viz. that in making a grant
in favor of a corporation of the church of England,
he fhould make ufe of a word in fome peculiar fenfe
of his own, and different from that in which he knew
they had been accuftom'd to underftand it. It may
therefore very reafonably be admitted that by orthodox minifters in this charter, theGrantor did " intend
" thofe of the Englifh church, *not* in diftinction from
" all other churches in the world," but in diftinction
from all thofe churches in the Englifh dominions,
(Scotland excepted) who diffent from the legal con-
ftitutional eftablifhment of England.

As pertinent to what has been here faid, the following paffage is inferted, with which Dr. Humphries
worthily concludes his hiftory of the Society. " In
" gratitude to the memory of the founder of this
" Society King William the third, it may not be
" improper to conclude this treatife with remarking
" to

" to the reader, the erecting of this corporation,
" was among the laft public actions of his heroic
" life. After having refcued the proteftant religion
" in Europe, and faved the church of England here,
" he did by this laft act, as it were bequeath it to
" his American fubjects, as the moft valuable legacy,
" and greateft blefling." But the Dr. adds—" to fay
" that the Grantees underftood the. term orthodox
" in this narrow exclufive fenfe, is to reflect upon their
" underftandings." As to their underftandings, it
would become him to fpeak with reverence of them,
as what he is not qualified to take the meafure of :
Nor is it any reflection upon them, that they fhould
underftand the term *orthodox* in fuch a limited fenfe.
For as the words orthodox and heterodox do in
their literal fignification import, the one a right,
and the other a wrong or different opinion, in matters relative to religion, fo, they who adhere to
the legal eftablifhed provifion, are ufually termed
orthodox, or perfons who hold a right opinion, and
they who diffent from fuch eftablifhment are faid
to be heterodox, that is, perfons who hold a wrong
or different opinion, whether their diffent arifes from
doctrinal points, or ritual injunctions. Nor had the
Dr. any occafion to wonder that his antagonift
fhould underftand the word *orthodox* as well capable
of the fenfe he had put upon it, fince it is ufed in
the fame fenfe in the hiftorical account of the Society as quoted by himfelf.† With as little reafon
does he charge that gentleman with not diftinguifh-
ing between *herefy* and *fchifm*, for he was not talking
of herefy, but of heterodoxy, between which
it feems this learned critic knows no difference.

D

AND

† Obferv. p. 101. 104.

, AND this feems to be a proper place to take notice
of another miftake that both the Dr. and his voucher
have gone into, relative to eftablifhments. The Dr.
does not indeed feem quite fo clear as his voucher,
that congregationalifm or independency are eftablifhed in New-England; yet he has faid enough to fhew
his inclination that the reader fhould believe it. Thus
in his 16th page he calls the minifters and churches
of New-England, the " eftablifhed minifters and
churches;" and a notable proof of their eftablifhment
he gives us at the 42d page, where he fays, that the
government of the Maffachufetts-Bay made a law
for the fupport of a learned and orthodox miniftry,
and this the Dr. calls a " civil eftablifhment of religion." I fuppofe the government will fcarcely thank
him for this interpretation of that law, which really
is charging them with invading the King's prerogative and eftablifhing themfelves : No fays the
Dr. in the next page, for the " acts which relate to
" the fettlement and fupport of the gofpel miniftry
" here, received the royal fanction, and therefore our
" churches *feem* to have a proper legal eftablifhment."
I believe if the Dr. held an eftate upon a title fo pre-
carious, as that of its being merely overlook'd, he
would be folicitous of obtaining a better confirma-
tion of it. Indeed he is fo modeft as only to affert
that " they *feem* to have a legal eftablifhment;" but
fince he knew that this was no eftablifhment at all;
it was perhaps not quite ingenuous to tell his readers that it *feemed* to be one.

IN his 72d page he afferts, that the Church of
England " is not eftablifhed here," which appears to
be introduced as another reafon why the New-England churches are eftablifhed. But now if it fhould
appear, that the church of England really is eftablifhed

blifhed here, and has been fo from the firft fettlement of the country; and that the churches (as he affects to call them) of New England fubfift here as the diffent- ing congregations do in England, upon no other foot than that of a toleration: I fuppofe the world will not look upon it very modeft in him to fpcak of the church of England in thefe colonies, as a *party*, a *faction, little epifcopal parties, fmall difaffected* and *difcontent- ed parties.*†— It will be proper therefore to fhew,

1. THAT what the Dr. calls the churches of New England are not eftablifhed in the colonies. And

2. THAT the Church of England is, and all a- long has been eftablifhed here.

THAT the New-England churches had no eftab- lifhment till the act of toleration took place, is evi- dent from their own confeffion; for fuch I take to be their fending an addrefs of thanks to King James the 2d. for a toleration of religion. Thus the affair is related by Dr. Douglafs. " Anno 1687. The " minifters of Maffachufetts-Bay colony, jointly fent " an addrefs of thanks to K. James 2d. for his in- " dulgence, or general toleration of religious opinions " and congregations; this was fent over and pre- " fented to K. James by Mr. Increafe Mather, he " and his conftituents, were not politicians, fufficient " to penetrate into the wicked and pernicious con- " trivance of that toleration." The Dr. adds in a note that " by this general indulgence popery was " craftily to be introduced; the colony of Plymouth " unadvifedly fent an addrefs of the fame nature."‡ If previous to this they had apprehended themfelves to be an eftablifhment, we can hardly fuppofe they would have fent a perfon a thoufand leagues to com- pliment that prince upon his granting the bleffing of a toleration. A

† Vid. Obferv. p. 55. 56. 57. 110. and in many other places. ‡ Sum. hift. & pol. p. 440. vol 1.

A fecond reafon to prove that the New-England churches are not eftablifhed here, fhall be taken from a letter of their Excellencies the Lords Juftices to the Hon. William Dummer, Efq; which is handed down to us by the hiftorian above mentioned, * and is as follows.

' Whitehall, Oct. 7. 1725.

' Sir,

' THE Lords Juftices being informed from fuch
' good hands, as make the truth of this advice not to
' be doubted, that at a general convention of mini-
' fters, from feveral parts of his Majefty's province
' of the Maffachufetts-Bay, at Bofton, on the 27th of
' May laft, a memorial and addrefs was framed, di-
' rected to you as Lieut. Governor and commander
' in chief, and to the council and houfe of reprefen-
' tatives then fetting, defiring that the general affem-
' bly would call the feveral churches in this province
' to meet by their paftors, and meffengers, in a fynod,
' which memorial and addrefs, being accordingly
' prefented by fome of the faid minifters, in the name,
' and at the defire of the faid convention, was con-
' fidered in council, the 3d of June following ; and
' there approved, but the houfe of reprefentatives
' put off the confideration of it to the next feffion,
' in which the council afterwards concurred.

' Their Excellencies were extremely furprized,
' that no account of fo extraordinary and important
' tranfaction fhould have been tranfmitted by you,
' purfuant to an article in your inftructions, by which
' you are directed upon all occafions, to fend unto
' his Majefty, and to the commiffioners for trade and
' plantations, a particular account of all your pro-
' ceedings, and the condition of affairs within your
' government,

* Sum. hift. & pol. vol. II. p. 337.

' government. *As this matter doth highly concern*
' *his Majefty's royal prerogative*, their Excellencies
' referr'd the confideration of it, to Mr. Attorney
' and Solicitor General, who after mature delibera-
' tion, and making all proper enquiries, reported,
" *That from the charter and laws of your colony,*
" *they cannot collect that there is any regular eftab-*
" *lifhment of a* NATIONAL *or provincial church*
" *there*, fo as to warrant the holding of convocations
" or fynods of the clergy, but if fuch fynods might
" be holden, yet they take it to be clear in point of
" law, that his Majefty's fupremacy in ecclefiaftical
" affairs, being a branch of his prerogative, does take
" place in the plantations, and that fynods cannot
" be held, nor is it lawful for the clergy to affemble
" as in fynods, without authority from his Majefty."
" They conceive the above mentioned application of
" the faid Minifters, not to you alone, as reprefent-
" ing the King's perfon, *but to you, and the council*
" *and the houfe of reprefentatives, to be a contempt of*
" *his Majefty's prerogative, as it is a public acknow-*
" *ledgment, that the power of granting what they*
" *defire, refides in the legiflative body of the province,*
" *which by law is vefted only in his Majefty.* And
" the Lieut. Governor, council and affembly inter-
" meddling therein, was an invafion of his Majefty's
" royal authority, which it was your duty as Lieut.
" Governor, to have withftood and rejected, and that
" the confent of the Lieut. Governor, the council and
" houfe of reprefentatives, will not be fufficient au-
" thority for the holding of fuch a fynod."
' Their Excellencies, upon confideration of this
' opinion, of the attorney and folicitor general,
' which they have been pleafed to approve, have
' commanded me to acquaint you with, and to ex-
' prefs

' prefs to you their furprize, that no account of fo
' remarkable a tranfaction, which fo nearly concerns
' the King's prerogative, and the welfare of his Ma-
' jefty's province under your government, has been
' received from you, and to fignify to you their di-
' rections, that you do put an effectual ftop to any
' fuch proceedings, but if the confent defired by
' the minifters above mentioned, for the holding of
' the fynod, fhould have been obtained, and *this pre-*
' *tended fynod* fhould be actually fitting, when you
' receive thefe their Excellencies directions, they do in
' that cafe, require and direct you, to caufe fuch
' their meeting to ceafe, acquainting them that *their*
' *affembly is againft law, and a contempt of his Ma-*
' *jefty's prerogative,* and that they are forbid to meet
' any more; but if notwithftanding fuch fignification,
' they fhall continue to hold fuch an affembly, you
' are then to take care that the principal actors there-
' in be profecuted for a mifdemeanour. But you are
' to avoid doing any formal act to diffolve them, left
' it be conftrued to imply that they had a right to
' affemble. This Sir, is what I have in command
' from their Excellencies to fignify to you.

 ' And I muft obferve to you, that the precedent
' quoted in the above mentioned memorial of fuch
' a fynod being held 45 years ago, falls in with the
' year 1680, and that the former charter, upon which
' the government of your province depended, was
' repealed by fcire facias in the year 1684, and the
' new charter was granted in the year 1691, from
' whence it appears, that if fuch fynod was holden
' as is alledged, it happened a fhort time before the
' repealing of the old charter, but none has been
' fince the granting the new one.
              I am Sir your moft humble fervant.
                     CHARLES DELAFAYE.'

LET us now compare Dr. Mayhew's opinion
with that of the attorney and folicitor general as
given us in the foregoing letter; and to make the
matter more plain to the reader, I will place them
oppofite to each other (as they are truly in themfelves) in feperate columns thus,

Dr. Mayhew's affertion that the New-England churches are eftablifhed here.	The Attorney and Solicitor General's opinion, and the determination of the Lords Juftices thereupon.
1. The government of the Maffachufetts-Bay, in the 4th of William and Mary, made a law for the fupport of a learned and orthodox miniftry; it is needlefs therefore to look any farther back, for a civil eftablifhment of religion here. Obfv. p. 42.	1. From the charter and laws of your colony (viz. Maffachufetts Bay) they cannot collect, that there is any regular eftablifhment of a national or provincial church there.
2. The acts which relate to the fettlement and fupport of the gofpel miniftry here, received the royal fanction, and therefore our churches feem to have a proper legal eftablifhment. P. 43.	2. The acknowledgment of fuch a power in the legiflative body of the province is a contempt of his Majefty's prerogative.

IT is really furprizing, that after fuch a letter as
this (of which it is fuppofed the Dr. could not be
ignorant) he fhould notwithftanding affert that the
New-England churches are eftablifhed. What becomes of his argument for a civil or legal eftablifhment, founded on certain acts of affembly, not
formally fet afide, and therefore fuppofed to be
confirmed by royal fanction, when the foregoing letter declares that the attributing fuch a power to the
legiflative body here is a direct invafion of his Majefty's prerogative. Whether the Dr. will incline to
difpute this point with the Lords Juftices, and prove
that the Attorney and Solicitor General did not underftand the colony charter, as he has attempted to
prove that the Society do not underftand theirs, I
am not able to fay. I fhall leave him to determine
that matter with himfelf, as he fhall think beft.

BUT

BUT perhaps the Dr. may be better fatisfied by an argument in his own way.—He lays it down as a rule for interpreting the charter of the Society, that " nothing can be fuppofed the objeft or any part of " the objeft of that inftitution, but what plainly " appears to be fo, from the very words of the " charter, even tho' it were certain that thofe per- " fons to whom it was granted, had at the very time, " fome farther views and ends in obtaining it, be- " fides thofe which are expreffed, or plainly implied; " yet the words of the charter itfelf mult determine " and limit the fenfe of the royal Grantor, and confe- " quently the legal power conferred—It was *only* for " thofe purpofes that are particularly expreffed, not " any private or fecret ones, which they might poffi- " bly have had in their own minds, that they were " incorporated." Let us now apply this rule to the charter granted to the Maffachufetts Bay. Nothing can be fuppofed the objeft or any part of the objeft of this conftitution, but what plainly appears to be fo from the very words of their charter, which very words muft determine and limit the fenfe of the Grantor. It was only for thofe purpofes that are particularly ex- preffed—Let the Dr. now read and examine the prefent colony charter, bearing date 1691, and point out to us the paffage or paffages where in exprefs words a power is granted of inftituting an ecclefi- aftical eftablifhment, or to ufe his own words, a civil eftablifhment of religion; but if nothing of this kind is to be found in it; if fuch a power be neither the objeft, nor any part of the objeft of the colony charter, it is more than probable that there is no fuch eftablifhment as the Dr. contends for exifting.

IF any thing further fhould be thought neceffary to confute the pretence of the New-England churches

churches being eftablifhed in the colonies, I fhall refer the reader to a letter fent from her Majefty and the Privy Council to the colony of Connecticut, Oct. 11th, 1705. See Doug. Sum. Vol. 2. p. 339.

IT has been now fufficiently proved that the New-England churches are not eftablifhed here. We will therefore inquire whether the church of England be not eftablifhed in the colonies.—This was before affirm'd.—I fhall now attempt to prove it. One would imagine indeed that there fhould be no occafion to enter upon the proof of a thing fo plain and evident as this is ; fince whatever difficulty there might be in determining this matter before, yet certainly there can be none at all fince the union of the two kingdoms, " becaufe, fays Dr. Douglas, " by the act of union of Scotland and England, it " is provided that the church of England govern- " ment in all the Englifh colonies was for ever " eftablifhed."† The fame author obferves in ano- ther place, that "by the articles of union of the two " nations of Great-Britain, May 1707, the church " of England is eftablifhed in perpetuity, in all the " territories at that time to England belonging."‡ I am a lofs how the Dr. fhould overlook fo plain a cafe as this, fo as to deny the eftablifhment of the church of England in thefe colonies, and to affirm that of the New-England churches. Poffibly the Dr. never examined the point himfelf, but took it upon truft from his voucher.

BUT tho' it is undeniably manifeft that the church of England is eftablifhed in all the Englifh colonies by the act of union before-mentioned; yet it may not be fo clear, that this eftablifhment actually took place before that time ; and altho' it is fufficient to

E   the

† Doug. Summary, vol. 1. p. 440, 441.   ‡ Do. p. 443.

the prefent argument, that the church of England
has been eftablifhed here from the time of the union
aforefaid ; yet for the fake of fuch as have not had
opportunity of examining this matter, I fhall lay
the cafe before the reader, as I find it already done
to my hands by a learned and judicious writer, in
a letter to the Rev. Mr. Thomas Foxcroft, printed
in the year 1745.

"The chriftian religion (fays this ingenious
" author) as by its evidence and intrinfic excellency
" it recommended itfelf to the Englifh government,
" fo it became by law the religion of the Englifh
" nation ; and the church of England likewife be-
" came by law their national church; and when
" any part of the Englifh nation fpread abroad into
" colonies, as they continued part of the nation,
" the law obliged them equally to the Church of
" England and to the chriftian religion. And the
" ftatutes for the eftablifhment of the fervice ordi-
" nation and articles of this church, made and con-
" firm'd before and at the union of the two king-
" doms, fettle and eftablifh it alike in *the dominions*
" of England, and in the realm it felf.

. " In the reign of Edward VI. certain bifhops and
" learned men by the appointment of the King, com-
" pos'd an order and rite of common prayer, and ad-
" miniftration of the facraments, in a book entitled,
" the book of common prayer, and adminiftration
" of the facraments, and other rites and ceremonies,
" after the ufe of the church of England. In the
" 3d year of his reign, an act of parliament was
" made (2d and 3d of Edward VI. c. 1.) entitled
" the penalty for not ufing uniformity of fervice and
" adminiftration of facraments, whereby it was enact-
" ed—That all minifters in any parifh church, or
other

" other place within the *King's dominions,* fhould
" be bound to fay and ufe the celebration of the
" Lord's Supper, and all their common and open
" prayer, in fuch order and form as is mentioned in
" this book, and none other, or otherwife.

 " In the fixth year of his reign, this book of com-
" mon prayer, was by order of parliament (5th and
" 6th of Edward VI. c. 1.) explained and perfeɛted;
" and a form of making and confecrating, Arch-
" bifhops, Bifhops, Priefts and Deacons was added
" to it; and by an act of parliament (entitled, uni-
" formity of prayer, and adminiftration of facraments
" fhall be ufed in the church) it was enaɛted, that
" the former act fhould ftand in full force and
" ftrength, for eftablifhing this book of common
" prayer, &c. as it was for the former book, and
" that if any manner of perfon inhabiting within *his*
" *Majefty's dominions,* fhould willingly and witting-
" ly hear and be prefent at any other manner or
" form of common prayer, &c. he fhould fuffer
" imprifonment, &c.

 " In the firft year of the reign of Queen Eliza-
" beth a few alterations and additions were made in
" this book of common prayer, and by an act of
" parliament (1 Eliz. c. 2.) entitled there fhall be
" uniformity of prayer and adminiftation of facra-
" ments, it was enaɛted, that all minifters in any
" parifh church, or other place within the *Queen's*
" *dominions,* fhould be bound to fay and ufe the cele-
" bration of the Lord's Supper, and adminiftration
" of each of the facraments, and all the common and
" open prayer, in fuch order and form, as is men-
" tioned in the 5th and 6th of Edward the fixth,
" with thefe alterations and additions, &c. and that
" every perfon inhabiting within the *Queen's Majef-*

" *ty's dominions*, fhould diligently and faithfully en-
" deavour to refort to the parifh church, or fome
" ufual place, where common prayer and fuch fer-
" vice of God fhould be ufed upon every funday,&c.

" IN the 13th year of Elizabeth, by an act of par-
" liament, entitled reformation of diforders in the
" minifters of the church : The preamble of which
" is, that the churches of the *Queen's Majefty's do-*
" *minions*, may be ferved with paftors of found re-
" ligion, it was enacted that no perfon be admitted
" to any benefice with cure, except he fhall firft
" have fubfcribed the 39 articles.

" IN the 14th year of Charles the IId. the book
" of common prayer, &c. was by the appointment
" of the King reviewed, and in convocation altered
" and added to, and prefented to his Majefty, and
" being approved and recommended by him to the
" parliament, was fubftituted in the place of that ap-
" pointed in the reign of Queen Elizabeth, and the
" parliament by an act (entitled an act for the uni-
" formity of public prayer, &c.) reciting that where-
" as the 36th of the 39 articles, is in thefe words,
" viz. That the book of confecration of Archbifhops
" and Bifhops, and ordaining of priefts and deacons,
" lately fet forth in the time of King Edward the
" fixth, and confirm'd at the fame time by authority
" of parliament, doth contain all things neceffary to
" fuch confecration and ordaining, &c. and there-
" fore whofoever are confecrated, or ordered accord-
" ing to the rites of that book, fince the 2d year of
" the aforenamed King Edward unto this time, or
" hereafter fhall be confecrated, or ordered accord-
" ing to the fame rites, we decree all fuch to be right-
" ly, orderly and lawfully confecrated and ordered,
" enacted that all fubfcriptions hereafter to be made
" unto

" unto the faid articles—fhall be conftrued and
" taken to extend, and fhall be apply'd for and
" touching the faid 36th article, and unto the book
" containing the form and manner of making, or-
" daining, &c. in fuch fort and manner as the fame
" did heretofore extend unto the book fet forth in
" the time of King Edward the fixth, mention'd in
" the faid 36th article. And by another paragraph
" in faid act, it is enacted, that the before-mentioned
" ftatutes, for the uniformity of prayer and admini-
" ftration of facraments, fhould ftand in full force
" and ftrength to all intents and purpofes whatfo-
" ever, for the eftablifhing and confirming this book.
" In the 5th year of the reign of Queen Anne,
" by an act of parliament (5. A. c. 5.) intitled, an
" act for fecuring the church of England as by
" law eftablifhed, it was enacted that all acts of
" parliament then in force, for the eftablifhment
" and prefervation of the church of England, and
" the doctrine, worfhip, difcipline and government
" thereof, fhould remain and be in full force for
" ever; and that every King and Queen fucceeding
" to the royal government of the kingdom of Great
" Britain, at his or her coronation fhould take and
" fubfcribe an oath to maintain, and preferve inviola-
" bly, the faid fettlement of the church of England,
" and the doctrine, worfhip, difcipline and govern-
" ment thereof, as by law eftablifhed within the
" kingdoms of England and Ireland, the dominion
" of Wales, and town of Berwick upon Tweed, and
" the *territories thereunto belonging*. And by the
" act of union of England and Scotland (5. A. c. 8.)
" this act was made an *effential and fundamental*
" part of the union,

I

! " I have now cited feven ſtatutes for the eſtab-
" liſhment of the Church of England in the domi-
" nions.—Theſe ſtatutes are all now in force, and
" do equally eſtabliſh and confirm the Church of
" England; her worſhip, articles and ordination, in
" the plantations and in England it ſelf." The
force of the argument which has been drawn from
them will doubtlefs prove ſatisfactory and convincing
to every one who obſerves, that every ſubſequent
ſtatute that has been cited refers to and confirms
thoſe that preceeded, and by that means throw their
united ſtrength upon the point here affirm'd ; ſo that
if plain direct poſitive acts of parliament have any
force in framing and confirming an eſtabliſhment,
the Church of England is beyond controverſy eſtabliſhed in all his Majeſty's colonies and plantations, and
therefore in the Maſſachuſetts Bay and Connecticut.

THE author does not recollect any thing that can
reaſonably be alledged againſt this concluſion, unleſs
the paſſage which was quoted before from the Lords
Juſtices letter, viz. " that from the charter and laws
" of this colony it does not appear that there is any
" regular eſtabliſhment of a national or provincial
" church here," ſhould be thought an objection.
If this paſſage ſhould ſeem to any one, to exclude the
plantations from any eſtabliſhment at all, whether of
the church or congregational denomination: It may
be anſwered ; It is not the intention of the ſaid letter to aſſert that there is no eſtabliſhment of religion
at all in the plantations ; but that *ſuch an eſtabliſhment is not to be collected from any powers granted
in the Maſſachuſetts charter, nor conſequently in the
laws founded upon that charter.* And ſince no ſpecial power or privilege of this kind was conferr'd
by the charter, it is evident that the ſtate of religion
in

in refpeŏt to eftablifhmcnts muft and does in faŏt reft upon thofe aŏts of parliament which relate to this fubjeŏt, and efpecially as they direŏtly include. all. his Majefty's dominions ; it being moreover an al⸗ low'd maxim not only that all laws made in the plantations contrary to the laws of England are ipfo faŏto void, but alfo that where a cafe occurs for which the laws of any colony have made no provi⸗ fion, fuch cafe fhall be determin'd by the laws at home. It appears then from all the aŏts of parlia⸗ ment that ever were made relative to eftablifhments, that there is an eftablifhment of the Church of Eng⸗ land in the plantations, and that authority allow'd and ratify'd by the reigning prince, was the proper authority to make an eftablifhment. "The King (under God) " is the fupreme head of the church " of England, and if he had not appointed an " ordinary over New-England, it would have re⸗ " mained under his own immediate ecclefiaftical " jurifdiŏtion as fupreme head. But it is well known " that his late Majefty, in the firft year of his reign, " did impower the Bifhop of London, under the " great feal, to exercife jurifdiŏtion over the clergy " in the plantations, which were not in any Diocefs, " but remained under the immediate jurifdiŏtion " of the King." †

We may now quit the fubjeŏt of eftablifhments, and proceed to confider the Dr.'s fourth feŏtion, which contains fundry " other things tending" (as he imagines) " to explain and confirm the fenfe of the " charter." The firft is, " the name by which this " corporation is diftinguifhed," viz. *The Society for the propagation of the Gofpel.* This has been fpo⸗ ken to before; it will only be neceffary to add here, that

† Vid. Letter above-mentioned, 1745.

that the Society have in their conduct acted agree-
ble to the import of this title, by sending millionaries into those colonies which the Dr. allows to be
proper objects of their institution, by sending others
to the Indian natives, and by appointing catechists to
the Negroes. In short, they have so far comply'd
with the import of this name or title, and with the
design of their institution, that the Dr. himself
is forced to confess, however unwillingly, " that the
" Society have *chiefly* sent their missionaries into
" those British plantations where they were much
" needed, according to the true design of their
" institution, and that they have thereby served the
" interest of religion."† But then he says, " they
" have deviated from the plan of their charter in
" some other respects," that is to say, they have
sometimes endeavoured to preserve men from falling
into infidelity by providing for them the means of
religion,—forgive them this wrong—Doubtless every candid person will allow that their institution
admits of the preservation as well as the extension
of the gospel, and whether the one or the other be
done, it must be done agreeable to the particular
profession and sentiments of those who are the un-
dertakers of this work. The Dr. adds, " for several
" years, he thinks about eight or nine, after the
" Society was founded, they sent no missionary into
" New-England, which may naturally be looked on
" *(he says)* as one argument that it was not origi-
" nally considered among those plantations which
" were supposed to stand in need of their charity."
But it is imagined that a better reason may be given
why few or no missionaries were early sent into
New-England, and that is, that few or no societies

or

† Obferv. p. 51.

or congregations, appeared at that time to aſk their charitable aſſiſtance. But afterwards frequent acceſſions of people of that communion from abroad, together with the effect of reading and enquiry at home, joined with the enthuſiaſm which at times prevailed, eſpecially after Mr. Whitefields appearing among us, and which drove many of the more ſerious and conſiderate people into the boſom of the church ; theſe things occaſioned ſuch an increaſe of the church of England, that the Society found it neceſſary, to allow a greater proportion of their aſſiſtance, as it was now earneſtly called for, and more apparently needed.

2. The next thing which the Dr. advances as limiting the deſign of the charter, is " *the common* " *ſeal of the Society*, which beſides a ſun in the up- " per part of the circle, has a ſhip within the circle " under full ſail ; on the prow of which ſtands a " clergyman with a bible in his hand which he ex- " tends to a company of naked ſavages on theſhore, " thronging to receive the bleſſing, juſt over whom " is a ſcroll implying theſe words *come over and help* " *us.*" It is not eaſy to imagine what this proof was alledged for, ſince it either proves too much, or elſe nothing at all to his purpoſe. If it was deſigned to prove that the *ſole* buſineſs of the Society according to their charter, was to carry the goſpel to the ſavages, this would directly contradict the charter, which declares the *primary object of their inſtitution to be the King's ſubjects*, but if it was brought to prove that the converſion of the natives was one part of the deſign of their inſtitution, this is no more than what we allow, and is agreeable to the conduct of the Society as well as their charter. Taking therefore the deſign of the charter in that ſenſe, in which the ſociety have all along underſtood it, and

F   agreeable

agreeable to which they have practifed, applying
themfelves both to theKing's fubjects and the natives,
and it very well agrees with the feal under confideration, but if applyed wholly to the natives which is
the ufe the Dr. feems to have bro't it for, inftead of
agreeing, as he fays it very well does, with the charter, it really is a flat contradiction to it.

3. The next thing alledg'd by the Dr. in fixing
the fenfe of the charter, is certain anniverfary fermons preached before the venerable Society, fome
paffages of which he has quoted, in fupport of his
opinion ; but this like the former inftance produc'd
by him, either juftifies the Society, or elfe is nothing
at all to the purpofe. For does not the Dr. himfelf reprefent the defign of their inftitution to be
that of preferving and propagating chriftianity among
the King's fubjects, and extending it alfo to the Heathen ? And has not this been the very practice of
the Society from the beginning ? And what do the
anniverfary fermons imply but certain exhortations
to purfue the feveral objects of their inftitution ;
thofe which the Dr. has quoted infift chiefly upon
one topic, while other fermons preached upon the
fame occafion enlarge on fome other branch of the
general defign? As to the particular paffages cited by
the Dr, he himfelf allows, that they do "rather coin-
" cide, with the ultimate, than the more immediate
" defign of the inftitution, and fo harmonize rather
" more perhaps with the feal and name of the So-
" ciety,than with the charter." What now are we to
learn from hence, but that the feal and name of the
fociety, which a little before he had produced to
explain and fupport his fenfe of the charter, do really not harmonize with it at all, but only with the
fermons he has quoted. So all he had been offering
before

before by way of proof, from the name and seal of the Society is now given up again, as being (what indeed it was) nothing to the purpose. This gentleman has a very strange method of proving and disproving, of asserting and giving up again: Sure he could never expect to arrive at any solid conclusion, by this wanton method of arguing. The truth is, those worthy gentlemen, who have preached the anniversary sermons before the Society, have not all of them confined themselves to the same topics, but as the institution of the Society comprehended several objects, some have enlarged more particularly upon one object, and some upon another, as they severally thought proper, but all within the general intendment and design of their charter ; and if the Dr. had intended to have drawn an argument from these annual sermons, in proof of the original design of their institution, he should have formed an abstract from them all, so far at least as they have enlarged upon different topics, and have given us the collective sense of the whole. But this indeed would not have served his turn ; for he himself says " He " is not insensible, that some of these sermons, es- " pecially within the last twenty years, have ex- " pressions in them of a much less catholic strain"; that is to say, they do not so well suit his purpose ; and in truth he has taken the liberty to treat them accordingly, that is with great indecency, as will appear to any one who consults his 13th, 14th and 15th sections, as well as many other passages of his book.

The author has now gone thro' the Dr's representation of the Society's charter, together with the several arguments he his advanced, to support the sense he hath put upon it, and has endeavoured 'to

prove

prove that they are altogether inconclufive ; whether he has fucceeded or not, muft be left to the judgment of the candid unprejudiced reader. In the mean time if the account which has now been given of the charter and inftitution of the Society be juft ; all the Dr's accufations of that venerable body, his charges of mifconduct, mifapplication of monies, and perverfion of the truft which they have taken on themfelves, fall to the ground ; and he has only to confider what reparation he ought in confcience to make, or endeavour to make, for the indecent liberties, and various abufe he has been guilty of towards them.

Here therefore the prefent examination feems to to conclude ; but as there are yet many things in the Dr's book, which the author conceives to be extremely exceptionable, he thinks it proper to take notice of at leaft fome of them.

It is a frequent fubject of complaint with him, that the Society have not done enough towards the converfion of the Indians, tho' by their public accounts it appears that they have omitted nothing in their power, to promote that good work ; nor have they been entirely without fuccefs. He is likewife much difpleafed, that more miffionaries have not been fent to thofe colonies, whofe religious ftate he thinks to be but little removed from heathenifm. What colonies he here refers to, we can be at no lofs about, fince he excepts none but thofe of Connecticut and the Maffachufetts-Bay. He allows for inftance that the Society might have fupported miffions in the colony of Rhode-Ifland with propriety enough ; and indeed they have done fo, and poffibly might have done more than they have, if they had not met with too much oppofition from a party fpirit. For inftance, The Society upon a reprefentation of the
great

great neceffity of a miffionary in theNarraganfet,particularly in South and NorthKingfton, at a time when there was no settled minifter of any denomination; fent thither Mr. Guy, Mr. Bridge, and afterwards Dr. Macfparran to officiate among them. To give a check to thefe gentlemens fuccefs, and left the inhabitants fhould receive religion, as it is taught in the church of England; one Mr. Torrey was difpatched thither, who had fo little pretenfions, and fo few adherents, that he could not find five perfons to give him a call (which I think the platform requires) and yet is officioufly continued there to this day, tho' his congregation, as I am informed by thofe who live in the neighbourhood, ufually confifts of fcarce twenty people.

Again, The Society open'd a miffion at Providence about the year 1722 or 1723, where at that time there was no settled minifter of the congregational perfuafion. But for fear thofe people fhould receive the benefit of religion agreeable to the church of England, a congregational minifter was foon fent thither, and as it is faid, even forc'd upon the people, who refufed to pay any thing towards his fupport.

Once more at Charleftown in the Narraganfet, an attempt was made by feveral church families in that town, to eftablifh a miffion for the benefit of themfelves, and the tribe of Indians in that neighbourhood (at that time about 400) to which attempt the Indians were fo well difpofed, by the labours of Dr. Macfparran a neighbouring miffionary, that the Sachem gave a piece of ground to erect a church upon, and a confiderable quantity of land befides, as a glebe for a miffionary. Accordingly a church was fet up, and the laudable defign in a promifing way, when one Mr. Parks was fent thither, to give

a

a check to the attempt, who by drawing off a party, and kindling a fpirit of enthufiafm among both Englifh & Indians in that town, totally difappointed and fruftrated the above defign.* Let the Dr. now reflect whofe fault it is, that this colony has been no better provided with miffionaries, and lay his hand upon his mouth, when it appears how indefatigable fome people have fhewn themfelves to fruftate the Society's attempts, even in thofe places where he allows they might laudably have employ'd their charity. Let it farther be obferved in anfwer to the Dr's principal objection, viz. " that the Society do not allow a " due proportion of their charity to the fouthern " heathenifh governments, nor to the Indian miffions." As to the former, feveral of thofe governments, heathen as they are, to their great honor be it fpoken, have made a handfome provifion among themfelves for the public worfhip of God, and therefore do no longer need the Society's help. And as to the latter, he is certainly a very improper judge what obftructions and difcouragements they have met with in their attempts to convert the Indians ; he therefore fpeaks at random, and with great want of charity when he fays they have neglected that part of their inftitution in order to propagate the church in N. England.

The Dr's fifth fection contains his account of the ftate of religion in N. England, before and fince the the incorporation of the Society. But this account in many things, can by no means be approved.

It is not the author's intention to call in queftion the religious character of the firft adventure s to N.
England,

* This lift might have been greatly enlarged, but it is an invidious fubject, which the author by no means delights in ; nor would have mentioned at all, if the Dr. had not cry'd out fo much about a party fpirit, and faulted the Society for neglecting this colony.

England, he doubts not in the leaſt but that they were ſerious well meaning people, and altho' labouring under ſome miſtakes and prejudices, yet many of them perſons of great wiſdom and underſtanding as well as piety. Nor will it be diſputed that they made " early proviſion for the public worſhip of God":* But how far their coming hither was occaſioned by their ſufferings and perſecutions at home, as alſo what their ſentiments were as to religious matters may deſerve farther inquiry.

In the mean time it may not be improper to take ſome notice of the great veneration the Dr. profeſſes for the memory of theſe our pious fore-fathers, who firſt came into this country, for the ſake of enjoying (as he ſays) purity of faith and worſhip. Could the Dr. have mentioned theſe good fathers without bluſhing, if he had reflected how widely he has departed from the faith which theſe good men profeſſed, and that as to the moſt eſſential doctrines of chriſtianity? ‡ Or muſt we take his appeals and harrangues of this kind to be mere grimace, or rather a deſign calculated *ad captum vulgi,* to raiſe a ferment in the minds of the people, who cannot help retaining, and that very juſtly, a value for the memory of their progenitors? Whatever their notions of liberty, or purity of religion amounted to, they certainly had no great opinion of *the learned Socinus* ; they entertained thoſe *orthodox* opinions, at leaſt concerning the divinity of the Son of God, which the Dr. has treated in ſo bold, as well as ludicrous a manner; and had he lived in their days, he

---

* Obs. p. 40.

‡ See his ſermons, on the terms of ſalvation—Of being found in Chriſt—Of juſtification by faith—and particularly his 2d ſer. on chriſtian ſobriety——Compare theſe with the doctrines taught by the early writers and divines of N. England.

he muſt either have enlarged his creed, or felt the effects of their honeſt reſentment. But tho' he has no right to take ſhelter under the merit of thoſe good men who are ſuppoſed to have firſt come hither for the ſake of enjoying a pure religion according to their conſciences, ſince he is departed from that purity of faith, whatever it was, which they profeſſed, as far as darkneſs is from light. Yet becauſe this ſtale pretence concerning the deſign of the firſt adventurers as to religious matters is artfully and induſtriouſly propagated among the common people who have not ſufficient opportunities of examining this matter, it will be neceſſary to give it a more particular conſideration.

Dr. Douglaſs acquaints us that " Robert Brown, a
" hot-headed young enthuſiaſtical clergyman, began
" anno 1580, to preach againſt the ceremonies and
" diſcipline of the church of England; he was per
" ſecuted or baited and teazed by the biſhops courts,
" he with ſome diſciples left England, and formed
" a church at Middleborough of Zealand in the
" Dutch low countries ; after ſome time this effer
" veſcence or ebulition of youth ſubſided, he re
" turned to England, recanted, and had a church of
" England cure beſtowed upon him, and died in
" that communion, anno 1630.

" A congregation of theſe Browniſts was form-
" in Yarmouth 1602, being harraſs'd by the eſta
" bliſhed church of England, with their paſtor they
" tranſported themſelves to Leyden in Holland ;
" here they became more moderate under the di
" rection of their paſtor Mr. Robinſon ; and from
" Browniſts changed their denomination to that of
" Independents : Being of unſteady temper, they
" reſolved to remove from amongſt ſtrangers after
" ten

" ten years refidence, to fome remote country in
" fome wildernefs, where without moleftation they
" might worfhipGod in their own devotional way."† *James*
Dr. Douglafs adds, that they " obtained an inftru-
" ment from K. James I. for the free exercife of
" their religion in any part of America"; but in
this article he is contradicted by Mr. Prince in his
chronology; who fays the utmoft they could obtain
was " that the King would connive at them, and
" not moleft them, provided they carry peaceably:
" but to tolerate them by his public authority; un-
" der his feal would not be granted."‡

Thus the firft effectual fettlement in N. England *firft fett*
was clearly made upon a religious account : But as *made on*
to the firft fettlers of the colony of the Maffachufetts *religious*
Bay, underftood as pofterior to, and diftinct from
that of Plymouth, they plainly acted as other men
ufually do upon like occafions, from hopes of in-
creafing their eftates, and providing an ample inhe-
ritance for their children. Having for thefe purpofes negotiated a fettlement for fome time, by a
Governor and Company refiding in England, they at
length thought it moft for the intereft of the propriety, that the feat of government fhould be removed to the country they were fettling. Accordingly Mr. Winthrop was chofen Governor, and he *Winthrop*
with his affociates embark'd on board fundry fhips,
of which the Arabella was admiral, with a defign to
proceed to America.

As it was now pretty generally known, that the
Plymouth adventurers had fet up a way of worfhip
different from the public eftablifhment of the nation,
it began to be fufpected and reported, that this new

G   company

† Sum. Hift Polit. Vol I. p 369.   ‡ Prince's Chronolo p. 57.
See alfo p. 53, 60.

company had a purpofe of the fame nature, as foon as they fhould arrive in America. This came to the ears of Governor Winthrop and his affociates, while they lay wind-bound at Yarmouth, and it gave them great uneafinefs, as well it might, to lie under the odium of this flander, and occafioned their writing the following letter for their own exculpation before they put to fea, viz.

Extract of a letter directed to the Bifhops and Clergy and people of the Church of England, from on board the Arabella, April 7, 1630.

For obtaining their prayers, and the removal of fufpicions and mifconftruction of their intentions.*

—" *WE befeech you therefore brethren by the mercies of the Lord Jefus, to confider us as your brethren, ftanding in very great need of your help, and earneftly imploring it. And however your charity may have met with fome occafion of difcouragement through the mifreport of our intions, or through the difaffection, or indifcretion of fome of us, or rather among us ; (for we are not of thofe that dream of perfection in this world) yet we defire you would be pleafed to take notice of the principals and body of our company, as thofe who efteem it our honour to call the church of England, from whence we rife, our dear mother ; and we cannot part from our native country, where fhe fpecially refideth without much fadnefs of heart and many tears in our eyes ; ever acknowledging, that fuch hope and part as we have obtained in the common falvation, we have received in her bofom, and fucked from her breafts. We leave her not therefore as loathing that milk, wherewith we were nourifhed*

---

* Prince's Chron. p. 205.

" *nourished there, but blessing God for the parentage*
" *and education, as members of the same body, shall*
" *always rejoice in her good, and unfeignedly grieve*
" *for any sorrow that may ever betide her,and, while*
" *we have breath.sincerely desire and endeavour the con-*
" *tinuance, and abundance of her welfare, with the*
" *enlargement of her bounds, in the kingdom of*
" *Christ Jesus.*—Be pleased therefore rev'd fathers
" *and brethren* to help forward this work now in
" hand——&c.   Signed by,
  JONH WINTHROP, Govr.
  THOMAS DUDLEY, Dep. Gov.
  Sir RICHARD SALTONSTALL.
  ISAAC JOHNSON.
  Rev. GEORGE PHILLIPS.
  WILLIAM CODDINGTON, ⎫ Efq'rs.
  CHARLES FINES,   ⎭

Previous to any application of the foregoing letter it may be proper to obferve, that Mr. Prince in
his chronology gives teftimony that thefe *pious peo-*
ple were profeffed members of the church of England.
" For the information (fays he) of the prefent age
" as well as pofterity, they (this colony of pious
" people) were of a denomination fomewhat diffe-
" rent in thofe early times from them of Plymouth
" —they were 'till now," (that is, after their arrival
in N. England) " profeffed members of the church
" of England." *

From the foregoing letter and teftimony it is evident, that whatever the cafe was at other places,and
with regard to other adventurers, the firft fettlers of
the Maffachufetts-Bay at leaft,thofe pious good men,
who left " the fair cities, villages, and delightful
". fields of Britain, for the then inhofpitable fhores,
             " and

---

* Prince's chronol. p. 213.

" and defarts of America" did not do it from any difguſt they had taken at the eſtabliſhed religion of their country ; but from quite other motives.——— They poſitively declare their veneration for the eſtabliſhed church, that they *eſteem it their honour to call her their dear mother*, that they *cannot part from the place of her ſpecial reſidence without much ſadneſs of heart, and many tears in their eyes*, they acknowledge that *the hope they have obtained in the common ſalvation, they received in her boſom, and ſuck'd from her breaſts*. They declare *they do not loath the milk with which they have been* thus *nouriſhed, but bleſs God for this their parentage and education*, that *their intentions have been miſreported ;* that *while they have breath, they will* SINCERELY *endeavour the continuance and abundance of her welfare, with* THE ENLARGEMENT OF HER BOUNDS, *in the kingdom of Chriſt Jeſus.*

After ſuch an explicit declaration as this, written and ſigned with their own hands, how can the Dr. pretend that theſe men were aggrieved at home, that they " came hither chiefly on account of their ſuf- " ferings for non-conformity," that " they fled hi- " hither as to an aſſylum from epiſcopal perſecuti- " on " *? Is the foregoing the language of the perſecuted, of men ſuffering for conſcience ſake ? In an honeſt and ſerious view, what foundation had he for calling upon people to " reflect on what their " fore-fathers ſuffered from the mitred lordly ſuc- " ceſſors of the fiſhermen of Galilee" ? What truth in ſaying that this " occaſioned their flight into this " weſtern world" ? Did our pious fore-fathers " throw themſelves into the arms of Savages and " Barbarians, to be delivered from the unholy zeal " and

* Obs. p. 39.

" and oppreffions of thefe lordly men, countenanc'd
" by fcepter'd tyrants "? * And would they at the
fame time earneftly afk the affiftance and prayers of
thefe lordly oppreffors, and openly acknowledge the
fpiritual benefits they had received from them? Read
my dear countrymen, read the words of our pious
fore-fathers, in the above letter, and compare them,
with this author's licentious harangue, and pretended
vindication of them, and fee with your own eyes
whether the fpirit of the one and the other have the
leaft fimilitude. In fhort either thefe pious good
men, were honeftly attach'd to the church of England, and ferious members of her communion, or
they were not; the Dr. affirms they were diffenters, they themfelves declare, that they were faithful
fons and children of the church, *educated in her bofom, nourifb'd at her breafts, bleffing God for this
their education, promifing to feek her welfare, with
the enlargement of her bounds* : From hence then
one of thefe two things muft unavoidably follow ;
either that they were dreadful prevaricators withGod
and man, or elfe that they are fadly abufed and flan-
dered, when contrary to their own exprefs declaration they are faid to have been diffenters, driven hither by the oppreffions and perfecution of the church
of England. If the former was the cafe, let us no
more boaft of them as pious good men ; If the latter, let the Dr. confider, what recompence he can
make to the memory of thefe men, for abufing them
with the opprobious charge of fectarifm and hypo-
crify.

And this feems to be a proper place to take notice of a reflection which the Dr. very liberally be-
ftows upon the eftablifhed church of England, which
he

* Obs. p. 155.

he calls " a cruel perfecuting church"* and fays
" the firft fettlers of the country were perfecuted
" out of England by the eftablifhed church."§ And
again, " is it not enongh" (fays he) " that they
" perfecuted us out of the old world? will they pur-
" fue us into the new"? ‡ And a few lines after he
fpeaks of the danger of being " confumed by the
" flames, or deluged in a flood of epifcopacy". A
ftranger would perhaps be led by this manner of
expreffion to conceive, that not only fire and faggot
were plentifully employed in England for extirpating
diffenters,but alfo that the Dutch method of knuting
was ufed towards them for the fame purpofes. Thefe
that have been mentioned are but a few, out of many, very many bitter terms he has thought proper
to beftow upon a proteftant church, univerfally ve-
nerated abroad, and generally efteemed the bulwark
and glory of the reformation ; a church remarkable
for its tendernefs, and kind reception of foreign pro-
teftants, when thefe have been obliged to fly from
their native countries on account of real perfecution.

I am forry the Dr. has made it neceffary to enter
upon a fubject fo invidious as this, and which lies
fo open to abundant recrimination. The author is
unwilling to renew the memory of thofe feverities,
that were too commonly practiced by all parties in
the laft century, and which feem rather owing to
the temper of the age, and the miftaken maxims of
policy then prevailing, than to have been the confequence of religious principles. The church of
England, confidered as fuch, has nothing in its conftitution, that either neceffitates or warrants a perfecuting temper ; and if any improper feverities have
at any time been ufed by the government, in fupporting

* Obf. p 40.　§ p 46.　‡ p 156.

porting the eſtabliſhed religion of the nation ; they certainly were as foreign to the principles of that church, as they are to chriſtianity in general. Will this gentleman allow that the perſecutions and op- preſſions exerciſed by the Preſbyterians, Indepen- dents, or by what name ſoever he chuſes to have them diſtinguiſhed, at a time when they had the govern- ment in their hands, were the natural and proper effect of the religious principles of thoſe denomina- tions? And yet a great number of the moſt cele- brated preachers of thoſe times, warmly inveighed againſt allowing even a toleration to ſuch as pro- feſſed the church of England, expoſtulating with the civil government upon that account, repreſenting ſuch an indulgence as a great ſin, a betraying the cauſe of Chriſt, and frequently uſing, or rather per- verting that expreſſion in the Goſpel, *compel them to come in.* Nay did not the violation of liberty and the rights of conſcience riſe to that height, as to prohibit by an ordinance under the penalty of five pounds ſterling, the uſe of the common prayer, even in the moſt private manner, in a perſon's own houſe? For a ſecond offence ten pounds, for the third one years impriſonment. * Should the ſeverities exerciſed

* And it is further hereby ordained by the ſaid Lords and Commons, that if any perſon or perſons whatſoever ſhall at any time or times hereafter uſe, or cauſe the aforeſaid Book of Common Prayer to be uſed, in any Church, or Chappel, or publique Place of worſhip, *or in any private place or family,* within the Kingdom of England, or Dominion of Wales, or Port & Town of Barwicke, that then every ſuch perſon ſo offending therein, ſhall for the firſt offence forfeit and pay the ſumme of five pounds of lawful Engliſh money. for the ſecord offence the ſumme of ten pounds. and for the third offence ſhall ſuffer one whole year's impriſonment without baile or mainprize. Vid. Ord. of Lords and Commons 23d Auguſt 1645. printed at the end of the Directory. The not uſing or depraving the ſaid Directory is by the ſame Ordinance made penal. And it is further hereby or aired that every miniſter which ſhall not henceforth purſue and obſerve the Di- rectory

exercifed towards the Quakers in the Maffachufetts-
Pay, (whom by the way the Dr. by an awkward
piece of flattery endeavours to complement with
his good opinion†) when by fines, imprifonment
and death of fome, ‡ the reft were obliged to take
refuge in a neighbouring government ; fhould thefe
feverities be attributed, not to particular indifcrete
men, but charged as a confequence of congregational principles, would this be thought a fair or generous conclufion ? yet thefe and a thoufand inftances befides, the effects of an indifcrete and wrong
pointed

rectory for publique worfhip, according to the true intent and meaning
thereof, in all exercifes of the publique worfhip of God within this
Realme of England &c. fhall for every time that he fhall fo offend,
lofe and forfeit the fumme of fourty fhillings of lawful Fnglifh money.
And that what perfon foever fhall with intent to bring the faid Directory into contempt and neglect, or to raife oppofition againft it,
preach, write, print, or caufe to be written or printed any thing in
the derogation or depraving of the faid Book, or any thing therein
conteyned, or any part thereof, fhall lofe and forfeit for every fuch
offence, fuch a fumme of money, as fhall at the time of his conviction,
be thought fit to be impofed upon him, by thofe before whom he
fhall have his trial, provided that it be not lefs than five pounds,
nor exceeding the fumme of fifty pounds.

† Obf. p. 50.

‡ Anno 1656 By a law of the province of Maffachufetts-Bay it was
enacted ; None of that curfed fect of hereticks lately rifen up in the
world, which are commonly called Quakers, are to be imported :
Penalty upon the matter £ 100 per peice, and 40f. per hour for any
other perfon harbouring or entertaining them. 1658 a Quaker con-
victed fhall be banifhed upon pain of death. Sum. Hift. Polit. Vol I,
p. 436. Again in p. 448 Some laws were made againft the im-
portation of Quakers and their proceedings — they were fubjected to
fines, imprifonments, whipping, cropping of ears (1658 three Quakers
had their ears cropt) and banifhment, and by act of affembly upon
their return from banifhment 1659 and 1660, three or four Quakers
fuffered death. This in courfe occafioned a national clamour, and
the pains of death were exchanged into thefe of being whipt, only
through three towns at the carts tail : But upon further complaints
home King Charles II in Council, by order, Sept. 9 h 1661, required the accufed to be fent home for trial, and all penal laws relating
to Quakers to be fufpended.

pointed zeal, might be mentioned by way of recrimination. Will the Dr. allow that if any of the
denominations, Prefbyterian, Independent, or Congregational, had now the power of government in
their hands, they would put on the fame oppreffive
temper?—Turely he will not.—Nor does he find
the church of England at this day praƈtifing any of
thofe fevcrities wherewith he labours to affright and
prejudice people againſt her. No eſtablifhment in
the chriſtian world, is more gentle, or allows greater
liberties to thofe who diffent from it, than the
church of England. Even the Dutch, who are
thought to afford as great liberty to confcience as
any chriſtian ſtate, are never known to admit any
perfons into civil offices, who do not conform to
the legal worfhip, which, altho' it be a reafonable
caution, is yet more than the Englifh government
are nice in exaƈting.

WHATEVER may be the temper of particular
men, it is pretty certain that at this time of day, all
parties difclaim thofe feverities which have formerly
been too much indulged; the people of New-England in particular, have fpecial reafon to be careful
how they countenance thofe who would promote
fuch a difpofition (to which fome may think the
Dr's manner of writing upon this occafion has no
fmall tendency) lcft the fame effeƈt fhould refult
from it, which has once been the confequence of
fuch a conduƈt in the province of the Maffachufetts
Bay; perfecution of their fellow chriſtians having
been one principal article which occafioned the va-
cating their former charter.† It was obferved, that
this Gentleman's writings have a tendency to ſtir
up mifaffeƈtion and a party fpirit (which are the
G   natural

† Sum. hiſt. & pol. vol. I. p. 412.

natural fore-runners of perfecution, where there is power to execute it) this was not fpoken at random, as will appear from the following paffages——
" When we confider—what might probably be the
" fad confequence, if this growing party" (the church
of England) " fhould once get the upper hand here,
" and a major vote in our houfes of affembly : (in
" which cafe the church of England might become
" the eftablifhed religion here; tefts be ordained as in
," England, to exclude all but conformifts from pofts
" of honor and emolument ; and all of us be taxed
" for the fupport of bifhops and their underlings)"‡

Now not to mention that the Church of England is already eftablifhed here, and tefts already ordained and in many cafes required, as they are in England; without any of thofe frightful confequences with which he labors to terrify the vulgar ; let it only be obferved that the plain import of this whole paffage is to perfuade people to unite in excluding thofe of the Church of England, not only from all pofts of honour and emolument, but even from the common rights and privileges of natural born fubjects; a fcheme fo notorioufly factious and unjuft, fo evidently tending to divide and alienate the minds of his Majefty's good fubjects from each other, that all wife and good men muft look upon it with indignation and contempt.

Dr. Douglafs tells us in his Summary, that " by
" an ancient law of the Maffachufetts province, none
" were allowed to be freemen but thofe who were
" church members, that is (fays he) of the indepen-
" dent or congregational religious mode ; and that
" only freemen were capable of voting in civil af-
" femblies." Upon which he remarks. " This was
" too

‡ Obferv. p. 155, 156.

" too narrow and confin'd, perhaps more fevere than
" ever was practifed by the Church of England in its
" moft bigotted and faulty periods."† To be fure a
greater infringement upon Englifh liberty was never
attempted; fuch a law might well therefore be repealed, as it foon was upon the King's letter in 1662.‡
And yet this is the very thing which the Dr. in the
foregoing paffages feems de firous of eftablifhing, not
by a law indeed, the legiflature are too wife and juft
to hearken-to infinuations fo fatal to liberty, but by
raifing fuch a violent fpirit of oppofition in the people as may anfwer the fame end. Let any man read
the virulent paffage now under confideration from
page 155 to 157, and having weighed the temper and
fpirit of it, let him turn to page 175, and obferve
the fame man declaring, that " he is far from de-
" firing to inflame the paffions of any one fect or
" party againft another:" and when he has done
this let him wonder. It is not expected he fhould
reconcile them, the author would not put the Dr.
himfelf upon fo impoffible a tafk as this.

SHOULD the Church of England prevail in New
England he is afraid we fhould " all be taxed for the
" fupport of *Bifhops and their underlings.*" This
was certainly too weak an infinuation for one who
writes himfelf D. D. and rather difcovers the writer's
paffion than his judgment. Even the loweft of the
people, are too much of *phylofophers and divines*, to
be taken in at this time of day, by fuch mean artifice
as this; but it was defigned to beget a prejudice in
the minds of the people againft epifcopacy, at which
he takes all occafions to exprefs his diflike; and indeed his beft friends muft wifh that he had done no

more ;

---

† Sum. hift. & pol. p. 432. ‡ Tho' the Dr. fays no acts of uniformity ever took place here, fo far as he has learnt, p. 94 of Obferv.

more; but when he fuffers himfelf to treat that whole venerable order, with an indecency of expreffion, which would be quite unbecoming if it were offered to the loweft of mankind, let the impartial reader judge from what temper it muft proceed.

THE Dr. could not be ignorant that epifcopal government generally obtained thro' all ages of the chriftian church; that it takes place at this day in almoft all the chriftian world; that the proteftant churches abroad, who are not fo happy as to live under this form of church government, do yet exprefs the higheft reverence and efteem of it; it would therefore doubtlefs have been more becoming to have exprefs'd his diflike in terms of greater modefty than he has ufually done in this and many other of his writings, of an order fo generally held in veneration. Even the admired Calvin and Beza have highly applauded the epifcopal hierarchy of England, as appears by their letter to Queen Elizabeth; the Archbifhop of Canterbury, and others. They pray heartily to God for the continuance and prefervation of it, bewail their own unhappinefs in the want of it, and mention it as their unavoidable misfortune to be without it. As to Calvin, altho' he juftly objects to that univerfal fupremacy claimed by the fee of Rome, as ufurping the prerogative of Chrift, he would not believe that any man could oppofe the epifcopal hierarchy; but (fays he, fpeaking of the Romifh church) " If they would fhew us fuch an
" hierarchy, in which the Bifhops might fo prefide,
" as not to refufe fubjection to Chrift, but depend
" upon him as their only head, and refer themfelves
" to him, then truly I will confefs that they de-
" ferve to be anathematized, if any fuch men fhall
" be, who refufe to reverence it, and fubmit to it
" with

" with the utmoſt obedience."† To the ſame purpoſe alſo does Beza exprefs himſelf. " But if any
" there be (which truly you will ſcarce perſuade me
" to believe) who rejeċt the whole order of Biſhops;
" God forbid that any man in his right mind ſhould
" aſſent to their madneſs."‡ And particularly declares that it was never his intention to oppoſe the
hierarchy of the Church of England which " ſingu-
" lar bleſſing of God he deſires ſhe may enjoy, and
" wiſhes it may be perpetual."§ If foreigners could
ſpeak with ſo much reſpeċt and reverence of this venerable order; how great a want of decency does it
imply in a ſubjeċt of this nation, who owes his liberty and every privilege he enjoys to the indulgence
of that very conſtitution which appoints them, how
indecent is it, I ſay, to ſpeak of them in ſuch opprobious terms as he has done in theſe obſervations, and
in many other of his writings, of which the reader
will hereafter find a ſpecimen ?

·Nor is it the venerable order of Biſhops only,
which this writer has treated with ſuch unbecoming
freedom. Every part of the eſtabliſhed eccleſiaſtical
conſtitution ſeems to provoke his diſpleaſure ; but
nothing raiſes his anger more, than that the Society
ſhould encourage the uſe of the liturgy in New England ; his contemptuous ridicule of which, makes the
greateſt part of his 14th ſeċtion. THIS,

† Talem ſi nobis hierarchiam exhibeant, in quâ ſic emineant epiſ-
copi, ut Chriſto ſubeſſe non recuſent, et ab illo tanquam unico
capite pendeant, et ad ipſum referantur, tum verò nullo non ana-
themate dignos fatear, ſi qui erunt qui non eam revereantur, ſum-
mâque obedientiâ obſervent. Calvin de neceſſitate eccleſ. reform.

‡ Si qui ſunt autem (quod ſanè mihi non facilè perſuaſeris) qui om-
nem epiſcoporum ordinem rejiciant, abſit ut quiſquam ſatis ſanæ
mentis furoribus illorum aſſentiatur. Beza ad Tractat. de miniſt.
ev. Grad. ab Hadrian. Sarav. Belga editam. c. 1.

§ Fruatur ſanè iſtâ ſingulari Dei beneficentiâ, quæ utinam ſit ill.
perpetua, ibid c. 18.

THIS, so far as it is an argument has been urged by him, oftentimes before, and implies that he thinks the Society, have no right by their charter to support a public religion in New-England, especially to the neglect of the Indians and the southern *heathenish* governments; for if they have a right to support religion in New-England at all, he allows it is natural to expect they should do it in their own way, and according to their own sentiments.† To this it has already been replied, that New-England containing a great many negro slaves that are still heathen, a great many freethinkers and other misbelievers, besides a great number of people from Europe educated in, and seriously attach'd to the Church of England, is directly in the most literal sense, one object of the Society's charity agreeable to their charter. And that they have also given their attention to the bordering heathen, and to those other governments which he esteems little better than heathen, in such proportion as they (whom he allows to be proper judges in this case) have found encouragement to hope for success.

As to the liturgy considered in another light, and as the object of his particular aversion, without entring into any direct vindication of it; it may be no improper rebuke to his licentious freedom upon this subject, to remark, that the whole christian church from the beginning has made use of liturgies in the public worship of God, as appears from the several forms of this kind which are still extant: And the foreign reformed churches at this day, have not only each of them a public liturgy, but have given ample testimony to the excellency of that in use

† *Observa.* p. 12.

ufe in the church of England ; † which confidera-
tions ought at lealt to have check'd his unfcafónable
ridicule, and have taught him to mention with an
air of greater ferioufnefs, a fubjeƈt which the
chriftian world have agreed to venerate.

THE

† In the year 1661 Dr. Durell publifhed a fermon in defence of the
Englifh liturgy, fome copies óf which he fent to feveral the moft
eminent minifters of the reformed churches in France. From
whom he received the following anfwers.

From Monfieur de l'Angle, minifter at Roüen.

Roüen, ce 5. Decem. 1661.
Monfieur et tres honorè frere,
Je ne fai fi je vous ai remèrcié
de voftre excellent fermon--c'eft un
excellent prefent que vous m'aves
fait, vous le deves faire imprimer
en mefme volume que voftre Li-
thurgie Françoife afin qu'il lui
ferve d'Ange Tutelaire, et qu'il
l'accompagne,in fecula feculorum.

From Mr. de l'Angle, minifter
at Rouen.

Rouen, December 5. 1661.
Sir, my moft honoured brother,
I know not whether I have
thanked you for your fermon—it
is an excellent prefent you have
made me; you ought to have it
printed with your Liturgy in
French of the fame volume, to be
as its Angel Guardian, and to
accompany the fame forever.

From Monfieur Bochart, minifter of Caën.

De Caën, ce Decemb. 1661.
Monfieur & tres honorè frere,
Je vous fuis tres obligé des ex-
emplaires de voftre fermon——
Voftre texte eft tres bien choifi,
bien expliqué, bien appliqué.

From Mr. Bochart, minifter of
Caen.

Caen, December 1661.
Sir, my moft honoured brother,
I am very much obliged to you
for the copies of your fermon—
your text is very well chofen, very
well expounded, very well applied.

From Monfieur Gaches, minifter
of Paris.

A Paris, ce 8. Decemb. 1661.
—Je paffe à voftre fermon, qu'on
m'apporta il y à trois jours, et
que je leu d'abord avidement.
Si vous avies befoin d'approbation
apres celle du Chappelain de
voftre Evefque, j'y joindrois tres
volontieres la mienne.

From Mr. Gaches, minifter of
Paris.

Paris, December 8. 1661.
—I pafs to your fermon, which
was brought to me three days
ago, and which I forthwith read
with great greedinefs. If you
ftood in need of an approbation,
after that of your Bifhop's Chap-
lain, 1 would moft willingly add
mine to the fame.

Thefe were followed by letters of the fame purport from Meffieurs
Daille, the father and fon, both minifters of Paris, from Monfieur Tricot, Monfieur Rofel, and Monfieur du Vidal, all three
minifters of the reformed church of Tours.

THE author has now gone thro' every thing in the Dr's book which he looks upon to be material, i. e. which relates to the profeffed defign, or principal argument of it. If any thing has inadvertently efcaped him, which the Dr. thinks to be of confequence to his main argument, upon proper notice of it, he will readily wait upon him again. There are indeed fundry incidental reflections to be met with, but as they are foreign to the general argument, and efpecially as they have been honour'd with fome proper remarks in a pamphlet lately publifhed at Portfmouth in New-Hampfhire, the author does not at prefent think it worth his while to take notice of them.

To fum up the argument on both fides———The Dr's book is entitled " Obfervations on the charter " and conduct of the Society, &c. defigned to fhew " their nonconformity to each other." In profecuting this defign the Dr. has given us his, or rather Mr. Hobart's fenfe of the charter ; this fenfe he has endeavoured to fupport, by adducing the title and feal, and fundry fermons of the Society in confimation of it. After which, comparing the conduct of the Society with the defign of their inftitution, as he has plann'd it, he finds them to be inconfiftent, or to difagree with with each other. This is a fhort (and it is fuppofed) a juft reprefentation of the Dr's management of the prefent argument, which if he had purfued in a modeft manner, without fcurrility or abufe, no body would have blamed him ? he would have been intitled to a modeft and genteel reply. Whether he has obferved this method, let the unprejudiced reader judge.

THE prefent reply is intended to fhew that the conduct of the Society is not inconfiftent with their charter, nor yet with the title or feal, or the anni-

verfary

(65)

verſary ſermons preached before them. To prove this the author has endeavoured to ſhew, Firſt, That the Society have always had ſuch means of information, both in reſpect to the true meaning of their charter, and alſo in regard to the ſtate of religion in the plantations, that it is morally certain they could not have been deceived in regard to theſe points. 2dly. The members of which that Society is compoſed, are in general perſons of ſo reſpectable a character, that it is utterly improbable they would act contrary to their inſtitution with deſign ; and further that if they were inclined to do ſo, it would have been impoſſible to have ſucceeded in ſo iniqui‐ tous a purpoſe, becauſe their charter obliges them annually to ſubmit their whole tranſactions, to the examination of the Lord chancellor and chief juſtices of the King's bench and common pleas, who are purpoſely appointed by the Crown to ſee that the true intent and meaning of the grant be complied with. 3dly, The author has examined the charter itſelf, and compared the ſame with the actual con‐ duct of the Society, and finds that they have pur‐ ſued the ſeveral objects therein recommended, agree‐ able to their title and ſeal, and to the general purport of their annual ſermons.

In examining the charter he thinks it appears, that the Dr's interpretation of it cannot be juſt, inas‐ much as it renders it inconſiſtent with itſelf ; ſo alſo his explanation of the ſeal and title of the Society militates with his interpretation of the charter, and ſerves to prove his miſtakes as to both. His quo‐ tations from the anniverſary ſermons of the Society, as they relate to one object only of their inſtitution, muſt be look'd upon as a partial repreſentation, how‐ ever they do not at all interfere with what is allow‐

I   ed

ed to be the fenfe of the charter, or with their general conduct, and confequently are nothing at all to the purpofe for which they were introduced.

Befides this, the author has made a few cafual ftrictures upon fome of the Dr's incidental reflections, as they happened to fall in the way of the principal argument ; and he was the rather inclined to do this, becaufe the Dr's quarrel with the Society, feems really to take its rife, not fo much from any thing he faw amifs in their conduct, as from his inveterate hatred, and unreafonable difpleafure towards the church of England, which he flatters himfelf could not fubfift long in the country without the Society's countenance and fupport. And yet in this perhaps he is miftaken, fince the providence of God has more ways than one of fupporting his own caufe ; fo that if the Society fhould think fit to withdraw their affiftance (which they will hardly do the fooner for fuch obfervations as his) it is not doubted but that God would raife up other helps, or fome way direct to fufficient means for the prefervation of his church. It was the advice of a wifer man than perhaps either of us, to the jewifh council, when they were confulting how they fhould put a ftop to the preaching of the apoftles, and the early propagation of the gofpel ; " Refrain from thefe men, and let them alone : for " if this council, or this work be of men, it will " come to nought : but if it be of God, ye can- " not overthrow it ; left haply ye be found even to " fight againft God."

If the Society, either through mifreprefentation, or by any other means, have been led into any miftake in the management of any part of their truft, no man will think that the Dr's indecent and

abufive

abufive treatment of them is the way to incline
them to amend it. Had it not been better to have
improved upon the hint which he has quoted from
bifhop Burnet, and by this means have excited their
emulation ? or as the bifhop exprefles it " have provoked them to jealoufly" ? Mr. Hobart referring to
the fame paffage mentions fome great things that
have been done in regard to the converfion of the
Indians by the Society in Scotland for propagating
chriftian knowledge, (it is fuppofed by the care and
management of their commiffioners at Bofton) with
a fmall expence. * Suppofing the truth of this,
(which the author has no inclination to call in
queftion) every good chriftian will fincerely rejoice
at it, and pray God that they may ftill meet with
more abundant fuccefs. But then would it not have
been infinitely more ufeful, and have difcovered
more of a chriftian fpirit, if the Dr. inftead of abufing the Society for the propagation of the gofpel,
had employed himfelf in giving a particular account
of that other Society which has been thus remarka-
bly fuccefsful, e. g. What has been their certain fund,
what their cafual benefactions, from whom they receive
their money, and how it is expended, what miffionaries
they employ, at what places they are fixt, and what
are their refpective falaries, and laftly, what accounts
have been received from them as to the fruit of
their labours : Had he done this, in fome fuch plain
open and honeft method as the Society for propagating the gofpel have done, it might poffibly not only.
have provoked them to emulation, but have opened
to them fome new or more effectual methods for
rendring their pious defigns fuccefsful. Certain it is,
that no Society, whether incorporated or merely
                                                voluntary,

* Mr. Hobart's 1ft Addrefs p. 129.

voluntary, whose single aim and intention it is to promote the glory of God, in enlarging the kingdom of the Redeemer, have any reason to be ashamed of publishing their transactions to the world: On the contrary it seems to be a duty to do so, not only to prevent suspicion of ill and improper designs, but also that their *light shining* out with a clear unsullied brightness *before men*, others may be induced either to join with them and strengthen their hands, or be led to set on foot some other pious and charitable work of a similar kind to the further advancement of God's glory.

As to Indian conversions the author's opinion is, that the Rev. and worthy Mr. Wheelock's judicious scheme of educating such of the younger Natives, as may be obtained, among the English at a distance from their own homes, and then sending them back to their friends and countrymen, whether as missionaries or otherwise ; if it may be done in any considerable numbers, would have the best influence in civilizing the savage temper of those people, and preparing them for the reception of the gospel ; This good design therefore, as it deserves all encouragement, so it is pity but it should be universally known. Mr. Wheelock has indeed published an open and undisguised, as well as a modest account of his plan, and of the progress he has hitherto made in it, but since it has not yet' circulated so far as it might be wished, this little intimation is designed to promote its being more generally known.*

But to return from this short digression.—If the Dr. should complain, or rather (since he has no right

* The pamphlet referr'd to is intitled, A plain and faithful narrative of the original design, rise, progress and present state of the Indian charity school at Lebanon in Connecticut. Printed by R. & S. Draper, Boston, 1763.

right to complain) if his friends fhould complain in his behalf, that in the foregoing remarks, the author has fometimes ufed too great a feverity of expreffion, let them confider the provocation ; let them refleét on the indecent language, and various abufe, that the Dr. has poured out, not on fingle perfons only, but upon public bodies, upon the moft refpeétable charaéters, upon the eftablifhed religion of the na-tion, upon thofe who come over to, or embrace it in N. England in general as men void of all piety and goodnefs, * upon the moft facred doc-trines of our holy religion — let them I fay refleét upon thefe things, and then fay whether there was not an occafion for fome kind of rebuke. The author is very far from being fond of harfh and fevere epithets, he had infinitely rather examine fub-jeéts of controverfy with that *meeknefs and fear* which is prefcribed by the apoftle ; but even the meek and gentle fpirit of the gofpel not only allows, but alfo requires in regard to fuch licentious free-doms, as the Dr. has thought proper to ufe, that they fhould be *rebuked fharply*.

If any one fhall ftill think that the Dr's foible is reprefented in too ftrong a light, that he has not been guilty of all that indecent abufe in his writings with which he feems here to have been charged ; let fuch perfon examine the following fpecimen taken from his own writings, moft of them folemnly de-livered from the pulpit. It is hoped that it will ferve to fatisfy the moft incredulous, and befides it may ferve *to fhew the Dr. to himfelf*, and let him fee how far he is departed, I will not fay from the dignity of the facred office only, but from the fpirit of the gofpel.

And

* Obf. p 98.

And firft obferve the modefty of his exprcffions in regard to Kings whom he calls Scepter'd Tyrants. Obs. p. 155. and fays that

The greateft part of mankind now are and almoft always have been oppreffed by wicked tyrants, called civil rulers, Kings and Emperors. Vol. Ser. printed 1755. p. 426.

2ndly. Expreffions in regard to the eftablifhed church of England, its conftitution, Bifhops and clergy

An enormous hierarchy afcending by various gradations from the dirt to the fkies. Obs. p. 155.

An hierarchy refembling that of the romifh church, where *one great prelate prefides* over the whole, with all the inferior religious orders, the loweft of which are as it were trodden in the dirt. Obs. p. 79.

He fays that one of our Kings

was wheedled and duped to his deftruction by the furious

It is not improper to obferve that the Dr. is fometimes in a better temper than what is imply'd in the oppofite column

particularly when he declares that

he would not willingly and unneceffarily give offence to any perfons of that perfuafion (the church of England) Obs. p. 175.

That the main end he had in view (in writing his Obfervations) was — that of ferving the caufe of truth and righteoufnefs-- in diftinction from all private party opinions whatfoever. Obs. p. 174.

He declares that he is far from defiring to inflame the paffions of any one fect or party againft another ;

furious epifcopal zealots of that day. Obs. p. 157.

And mentions the bifhops before the revolution

The perfecuting antichriftian fpirit of many prelates before the revolution. Do. 157.

And in the foregoing page fpeaks contemptuoufly of

Bifhops and their underlings. p. 156.

In the page before they are ftiled

The mitred lordly fucceffors of the fifhermen of Galilee. Obs. p. 155.

In the 39th page he fays that before the revolution

\ Epifcopal perfecution was feconded by royal power ; which condefcended to be fubfervient to the views of domineering prelates. Obs. p. 39.

In another paffage he fays that

Their unholy zeal and oppreffions, *were* countenanced by fceptred tyrants, p. 155.

In which latter expreffion as well as many others of

another : fo far from it that he would fincerely rejoice to be in the leaft degree inftrumental of uniting them in the bonds of Chriftian charity, on the true plan of theGofpel. Obs. p. 175.

Has a great averfion to controverfy. Obs. p. 7.

When once providence fhall have put it in our power to live thus (peaceably that is in refpect to our enemies) — we are wholly inexcufeable—if we fhould turn afide to vain jangling amongft our felves,

of like kind he has reason he says to think that

He speaks the sense of the far greater, wiser and better part of the people in N. England. p. 154.

As to this I have better reason to think that he is widely mistaken, and that the greater, wiser and better part of N. England do entirely disapprove his censorious indecent and uncharitable temper.

Having thus treated the bishops, the church itself could not expect better quarter, and accordingly he has characteriz'd the church of England, the established church of the nation, of which the King himself is, under God, the head, which he loves and has sworn to defend, to be,

A cruel persecuting church,—Obs. p. 40. to which that he might preserve himself from the censure of civil authority he subjoins,

As that was before the revolution.

·We

selves, doting about questions and strifes of words, whereof cometh envy, strife, railings, evil-surmisings, and perverse disputings, instead of studying the things that make for peace, and the things whereby we may edify one another.

If we should heneforth live as becomes fellow-subjects and fellow-christians, in the fear of God, and brotherly love, &c. Serm. on the reduction of Quebec, p. 59, 60.

The

We may now pass to some expressions deliver'd by him from the pulpit, as contained in a sermon on the anniversary of King Charles's martyrdom. In the preface to which he speaks of Bishops and the clergy in general under the title of

Imperious Bishops and reverend Jockies.

And in the sermon itself they are stiled

Reverend and right reverend drones ; who preach but once a year, and then, not the gospel of Jesus Christ, but—some favourite point of church tyranny and antichristian usurpation.

p. 21. 22.

Speaking of the King, he says that

He supported that *more than fierce* archbishopLaud and the clergy of his stamp, in all their church tyranny and hellish cruelties. p. 42.

The opposite expressions are the language of one who says he would not bring a railing accusation even against the devil, tho' he were contending with him, much less would he bring such an accusation against his brethren.

Vol. I. Ser. X. p. 354.

I am far from intending (says the Dr.) to debase preaching by scolding, or bringing a railing accusation, even against wicked and ungodly men. Nor will I forget the apostle's admonition to Timothy, Rebuke not an elder [or aged person] but intreat him as a father : as I hope I have not forgotten what he immediately subjoins,

There
K

There feems to have been an impious bargain ftruck up betwixt the fceptre and the furplice for enflaving both the bodies and fouls of men. The King appeared to be willing that the clergy fhould do what they would—fet up a monftrous hierarchy like that of Rome—a monftrous inquifition like that of Spain or Portugal—or any thing elfe which their own pride, and the devils malice could prompt them to. p. 52.

Take a further fample of this Gentleman's meek fpirit and temper.

Some contend and *foam* and curfe their brethren for the fake of the athanafian trinity till 'tis evident they do not love and fear the one living and true God. Others you will fee *raging* about their peculiar notions of original fin, fo as to prove themfelves guilty of actual tranfgreffion.

fubjoins, and the younger men as brethren. Prac. Difc. on the earthquake, Serm. IX. p. 263, 264.

The oppofite are ftrange expreffions, to fay no worfe, for one who calls himfelf a minifter of Jefus Chrift.

Would not any ferious perfon imagine that the oppofite paffage would have been full as defcriptive (I know it would not have been quite fo rhetorical) if the words *foaming*, *raging*, *quarrelling*, *fury* and *bitternefs* had been omitted, or at leaft if fome fofter terms had been

tranfgreffion. About elec-
tion till they prove themfelves reprobates. About
particular redemption till
they fhew that they them-
felves are not redeemed
from a vain converfation.
You will hear others *quar-*
relling about imputed
righteoufnefs with fuch
fury and *bitternefs*, as to
fhew that they are defti-
tute of perfonal. About
fpecial grace, fo as to fhow
that they have not even
common. About faith
while they make fhip-
wreck of a good con-
fcience.

Serm. XI. Vol. I. p. 403.

It will doubtlefs be dif-
agreeable to the reader to
be any longer entertained
with expreffions and ob-
fervations fo utterly un-
becoming a minifter of
Jefus Chrift, or in truth
any other difciple of that
divine mafter. The author
will here therefore put an
end to the fpecimen with
the mention of a trifling
inconfiftency which this
otherwife accurate Gen-
tleman has fallen into in
the heat of his argument.

been fubftituted to ex-
prefs his difpleafure at
thofe who hold the doc-
trines he there mentions.

Mr.

Mr. Apthorp had observed that the religious state of the country is manifestly improved as to its speculative doctrines, notwithstanding the immoralities we lament and wish to reform. After spending several pages (viz. from 83 to 92.) to confute this position, the Dr. concludes as in the opposite column—.

It has been too common for people in New-England to express themselves in a manner justly exceptionable upon these points (i. e. the principles he supposes the Gentleman had referr'd to) Obs. p. 92. and in Serm. I. Vol. I. p. 16. He says it is one of the chief honors of the present age, that the principles of religion, particularly of religious liberty, are better understood and more generally espoused, than they have perhaps been since the days of the apostles; it were to be wished that practical christianity, had made progress in the same proportion.

THIS little contrast is left to speak for it self; but as to the forgoing specimen the author presumes the Dr's. best friends, must seriously wish that he had expressed himself, not only with more decency and respect, but more agreeable to the temper of the gospel: Others perhaps who have less tenderness for him, will also have less charity, and be liable to suspect that he deceives himself, when he professes a regard for that divine religion which disclaims all evil speaking, railing and reviling, and whose principal characteristic is love or benevolence, a principle which they may think he notoriously violates——Be that as it may, the author is of opinion that the

Dr.

Dr. has no room to complain of harſh or ſevere treatment, no not altho' it ſhould be more diſagreeable than any he has yet met with ; unleſs he will be pleaſed for the future at leaſt to treat mankind with more reſpect than he has uſually done, not only in his book of obſervations but even in many of his ſermons.

THE author cannot perſuade himſelf to conclude theſe reflections without expreſſing his aſtoniſhment, that any gentlemen, tho' of congregational principles, and much more that the reverend gentlemen who are the ſpiritual guides of that denomination, overlooking the Dr's attempts to undermine the fundamental principles of their faith, ſhould expreſs their approbation of this his performance, which in the conduct of it diſcovers ſo little of the meekneſs and gentleneſs of the goſpel. Can you, gentlemen, be ſo far blinded by prejudice or a party ſpirit, as tamely to give up thoſe eſſential doctrines for which you have hitherto laudably contended, and which once you eſteemed your glory ? Can you, I ſay, cheriſh and flatter the man, who has been labouring from pulpit and preſs to demoliſh the doctrines which your fore-fathers have handed down to you ? (while yet he pretends to venerate them) thoſe doctrines, which by way of eminence, you have been wont to ſtile the doctrines of grace ? †   Are theſe things · of leſs conſequence than an oppoſition to the church of England ? How is it then · that you have complimented the Dr. with your thanks (for ſo I hear many of you at Boſton have done) for his book of obſervations, who by his other writings, 'has been deſtroying the fundamentals of your faith ? Has he not been undermining the dignity and divinity of

the

† Vol. of Serm. printed 1755, paſſim.

the fon of God? ‡ Does he not deny and ridicule
the doctrine of juftification by faith? calling it
confufion and an unintelligible rant, † nonfenfe, ‡
gibberifh,‖ mere jargon, § a means of beguiling
unftable fouls to their deftruction, ‡‡ an irrational
unfcriptural doctrine, of pernicious tendency with
regard to the lives and manners of men.†† Does
he not difcard the notion of original fin, and brand
the doctrine of imputed righteoufnefs with the re-
proach of nonfenfe? And have you not, gentlemen,
implicitly countenanced thefe, and the numerous
other errors in doctrine which are fcatter'd up and
down his writings, by your unfeafonable compli-
ments for his late obfervations upon that venerable
Body of men the Society for the propagation of the
gofpel, &c. Will not ftrangers, will not every one
who fhall read the errors which this gentleman has
publifhed, naturally conclude, that you, gentlemen,
do abet and approve them, who have thus given
your fanction to this his laft, but not leaft injurious
performance?—I fpeak it with grief and concern,
are you fo carried away with a party fpirit as to
countenance fuch abufe and mifreprefentation of the
church of England, while you have not the courage
to rife up in defence of the Lord Jefus Chrift, and
the truth of his gofpel?—Remember who has faid,
" he that is afhamed of me and of my words, &c.
" of him fhall the Son of Man be afhamed when he
" cometh in the glory of his Father with the holy
" angels."

BUT

‡ See vol. I. ferm. IX. p. 267, 268, 291. Serm. X. p. 341, 342. Serm. XII. p. 417, 418. note, but particularly Serm. II. on Chriftian Sobriety, from p. 57 to 68.

† Serm. VII. vol. I. p. 173, note. ‡ Serm. VIII. p. 237. ‖ Serm. VIII. p. 249. § Do. p. 251. ‡‡ Do. p. 244. †† Do. p. 255.

BUT to return from this digreffion, if it may be called one.—Befides the errors in doctrine hinted at in the foregoing remarks, the Dr's reflection upon the Song of Solomon is fufficient to fhow how eafy it is for him to difcard even the facred canon of fcripture itfelf: Or perhaps it was introduced merely for the fake of the witticifm. It would difcover however both more wifdom and ferioufnefs to referve his drollery for fome lefs important fubject. But no witticifm, nor any thing elfe, will juftify the pernicious tendency of the doctrine of annihilation, to which he has given too much countenance in the following paffage. Speaking of fuch as die in their fins; " The utmoft they can hope for (fays " he) is to be annihilated after fuffering unutterable " torments: Tho' I do not affert, that they can, ac- " cording to the fcripture account, hope for fo great " a favor as even this would be, viz. to be utterly " blotted out of being! However it muft be con- " feffed that fome expreffions of fcripture feem, at " firft view, to countenance this fuppofition."‡ This will too greedily be catched at by thofe who have lived in fuch a manner, as to have no better hope in their death. It might not be amifs for the Dr. to take a review of his works, and expunge this and many other paffages which certainly have a threatning afpect upon the religion of Jefus Chrift.

BUT befide the ill confequences to religion, and efpecially among the rifing generation, which may not improbably follow from the principles he is labouring to propagate: If the government enjoy any privileges by virtue of their charter, which they are fond of retaining; one may be confident that the fpirit and temper of the Dr's writings, fo far as it can be fuppofed

‡ Ser. Vol. 1. p. 475. 476. note.

fuppofed they are publickly countenanced, will be attended with no favourable impreffions, where it is the intereft of the province to ftand in a favourable light. It were to be wifh'd that this were more thought of by fome well difpos'd people, who do not appear to be aware of the confequences, which fuch improper liberties may produce in regard to the civil interefts and privileges of that province.

As the author firmly believes that this is not the general temper of people in the colonies, fo it is hoped it will be received *at home* as the effect of this Gentleman's particular difpofition only, and that of two or three of his abettors.

To conclude, the author apprehends he has now *fhewn* the Dr. *to himfelf* (to ufe his own phrafe) and he hopes has alfo fhewn him to other people. The firft with a charitable view to his amendment, the latter with a defign to caution others againft being mifled. To thefe good purpofes, it will not be improper to pray, tho' in the words of the liturgy, " that God would grant unto us all, that we may " both perceive and know what things we ought to " do, and alfo may have grace and power faithfully " to fulfil the fame."

A LETTER

A short Vindication of the Society for the Propagation of the Gospel, &c. against the Objections, Mistakes and Misrepresentations of Dr. MAYHEW, in his Observations, on the Conduct of that Society.

By one of its Members.

In a LETTER to a FRIEND.

Dear S I R,

THE great difficulty I labour under in writing, must be my apology for writing very briefly, and attending only to the most material things.

It is too evident from the general current of Dr. *Mayhew's* performance, That, it is his aim to beget a prejudice, and an odium in his readers, against his antagonist, and against the church of *England*, and the Society, from considerations and reflections, either meerly personal, or ludicrous, and often trifling, and few of them, relating to the real merits of the cause ; which is a practice quite unbecoming a *just* writer, either in the critical, or moral sense of that character.

There is one grand imposition upon his readers, which runs through the whole, and is, as it were, the burthen of his song, in which, there is not the least truth, and for which, there never was the least ground, or foundation, as ever I could learn, viz. That the chief view and endeavour of the Society has been to convert presbyterians and congregationalists to the church, to the neglect of Negroes and Indians, and the *heathenish* colonies, as he calls them.

L   If

If they, or their miffionaries had done this, they would have had infinitely more reafon, and right in what they did, than the diffenters from the beginning had, in ufing all poffible endeavours, to promote factions, and difaffect people, to the eftablifhed church of *England*, in all quarters, and make all the profelytes they could, from her communion, to their confufed parties and fects, iffuing in downright rebellion : So that this, is alledged with a very ill grace, by one, derived from, and who is a violent abettor of that party.

It is true, every good churchman muft rejoice, when any of our wandering brethren, who have been drawn away, from the bofom and communion of the church, or educated in prejudice againft it, are reclaimed, and return to the unity of the church, and be glad to be inftrumental, as God in his providence gives them opportunity, in reconciling any of them : But, as the Society was not incorporated for that purpofe, nor was it ever their principal aim, I believe very few inftances, if any, can be produced, of any miffionaries beginning with any diffenter, with a view at reclaiming him to the church. I have been long knowing to the affairs of the Society, and know of no fuch inftances.

We have indeed been treated with great obloquy by diffenters reprefenting us, as little better than roman catholics, &c. On thefe occafions we have defended ourfelves, as well as we could : and can any body blame us for it ? And can any reafonable perfon wonder if this fhould fometimes prove the occafion of the converfion of fome fenfible honeft people ? Or if the mcer curiofity of others attending occafionally on our beautiful and inftructive fervice, fhould be the means of their being reconciled, when they fee, that it does not confift of extempore human invention, but is a wife and judicious collection from the holy fcriptures ? fo that, their very love to the fcriptures, has fometimes led them to love the fervice of the church.

But it is faid, That Dr. *Bray*, the father of the Society, reported, that in the *Maffachufetts* and *Connecticut*, there was no occafion for the Society to do any thing, as they were provided for, in the diffenting way :—I anfwer, I knew Dr. *Bray* very well, he was doubtlefs a very good man, and I
agree

agree to his report at that time, and fhould have made the fame report myfelf: There was then (except at *Bofton*,) but here and there a member of the chuich of *England*, fcattered about in thefe provinces ; and according to the conflitution of the Society, while there was no congregation of the church in thofe parts, the Society had no occafion to fend any miflionaries thither : But does it at all follow, that when there came to be fuch numbers of confcientious members of the church of *England*, as to make competent congregations for worfhip, being not well able to provide for a minifter themfelves, that the Society had by their charter, no right and bufinefs, to aflift in providing for them, meerly becaufe the diffenters in thofe provinces were already provided for ? Can any reafon be given, why a confcientious body of church people in thefe provinces, fhould not be provided for, as well as in any other province ?—You will fay, let them go to meeting, I anfwer, many of them were fo candid, as to go to the meetings, rather than no where, tho' it was very tedious and difagreeable to them, till they grew in numbers, fo as to make competent congregations.

Yea, but it is reprefented, That the origin of the church, in thefe provinces, has been generally owing to faction, difcontent with minifters, and about rates, pews, and the like, and tho' the church is the eftablifhed religion of our mother country, and in the act of union, is, (as Dr. *Doug-lafs*, his favourite author allows) eftablifhed in all the plantations ; he is pleas'd in his great good manners, to fpeak of her in thefe governments, under no better terms, than thofe of party and faction.

How much truth there may be in Dr. *Colman*'s account of the origin of the church, at *Newbury* and *Braintree*, I am not able to fay, and that fome individuals have had little better motives in conforming, than thofe mentioned, I will not deny, and perhaps fome of the miflionaries have not always acted prudently, and poffibly fome may have been in a few inflances too forward ; fuch things are common to frail human nature ; however, this I know, that the general rule and practice, where I am acquainted, have been, to fend male-contents, and perfons liable to cenfure, back, to make peace at home, before they came

over

over to us. But, suppose some things a little wrong, is it fit, that so respectable a body, as the Society or the church, should be reproached, with the forwardness, or misconduct, of a few individuals ?

Let me, however, give what I know to be generally a true account, of the origin of the church in these provinces.

The true causes, and occasions, of the being and growth of so many congregations of the church of *England*, in these provinces, are these.

1st. As the country continued to increase, and there were many accessions from *Great-Britain* and *Ireland*, there were among others, many of the established church, who came over to settle in these colonies, as well as others, so that there was 50 years ago, scarce a town of considerable standing, but what had some scattering among them, and in some there were several families : In *Stratford*, for instance, the first in *Connecticut* that applied to the Society ; there were at the beginning of this century about fifteen families, and five or six more in the nearest towns, that joined with them ; and in 1722, when the first mission was established, there were about thirty or forty ; now, on supposition that the first who settled in these provinces were dissenters generally, yet I know no reason why these lands should be thought so sacred to them, as to exclude the church, nor, why church people should not be at liberty, to settle themselves in these colonies, as well as in any others ? And if they do, who can deny, that they have as good a right to enjoy their way of worship as their neighbours ? And if they need, and obtain any charitable assistance, can any thing but envy and malevolence, make such a clamour against it ? But,

2. So the case has been, ever since church people settled in these countries, many dissenters have treated them with much clamour and contempt, and frequent disputings have arisen, which occasioned many to procure books, wherewith to defend themselves, such as arch bishop *King*'s inventions of men in the worship of God, the *London* cases, *Hoadley* against *Calamy*, arch bishop *Potter* on church government, and some *Hooker*'s ecclesiastical polity, and such like. And their thus defending themselves, occasioned many

many inquifitive candid diffenters to read thofe books, which reconciled them to the church ; fo that the diffenters them- felves by thus cenfuring, and difputing, have occafioned the increafe of the church, and I hope it may be truly faid, in a judgment of charity, many both of the original church people, and of the profelyted diffenters have been fincerely confcientious.—Dr. *Mayhew* indeed, and fome other diffen- ters, however differing in fome things, as much, (if not more) among themfelves, as either of them from the church, feem fo bigotted to their diffenting principles, in one fhape or other, and fo full of themfelves, that they fcarce know how to imagine, that church people, or any who differ from them, can be confcientious ; but furely, any candid and indifferent perfons, that know any thing of fuch great and good men, as *Hooker* and *Chillingworth*, muft allow, that it is poffible, for a church man, upon the foot of *Hooker's* ecclefiaftical polity, and *Chillingworth's* demonftration of epifcopacy, (to fay nothing of arch bifhop *Potter* and arch bifhop *Sharp*, and the many others) to be at leaft as con- fcientious, as any diffenters in their way' upon the foot of any of their various principles.

3dly. Another thing and what has of late chiefly occafioned the acceffion of multitudes to the church, was, the wild en- thufiafm that long obtained among themfelves, on which oc- cafion, their own managements were in many inftances, fo extravagant and ridiculous, as tended vaftly more, to drive their people into the church, than any thing we ever did to draw them over to it.— Particularly, that monftrous enthu- fiafm that was at firft mightily encouraged by themfelves fifteen or twenty years ago, in confequence of Mr. *White- field s* rambling over the country, once and again, who was followed by a great many ftrolling teachers, who propagated, fo many wild and horrid notions of God and the gofpel, that a multitude of people, were fo bewilder'd that they could find no reft to the fole of their foot, till they took refuge in the church, as their only ark of fafety. And many of thefe wild notions (to fay nothing now of the oppofite extreams of arianifm, focinianifm, and independent-whiggifm) continue among great numbers to this day, and have occafioned much hot contention among them in fettling minifters, and often

the

the proftitution of difcipline upon the meaneft trifles, which
have occafioned many people to conclude, that if they muft
feparate from their former brethren, who are in endlefs contentions and confufion, their beft way muft be to retire into
the church, which is in peace.—Now, thefe are all known
facts : Is not Dr. *Mayhew* then very difingenuous to con-
ceal them, and afcribe the being and increafe of the church,
only to petts and quarrels about pews, rates, and fuch trifling things, and to a meer fpirit of faction ?

But, it is pretended, great mifcheifs have befallen the
country by means of the church, (of which however, he
gives no proof) ; to this I anfwer, certain it is, that great
advantages have derived from it, even to the diffenters themfelves : it has occafioned a great increafe of knowledge, by
their reading many of our excellent writers, from whom
they have gained their beft notion's, and much greater
correctnefs, than they had, both in writing and fpeaking ; it
has provoked them to emulation, and it is certain, that
many of them have much better notions of God and the
gofpel now, than they had before, and have much improved
in the knowledge of the fcriptures and the evidences of
chriftitanity.—Certain it is, that they are now, much beyond what they were, fifty years ago, and as certain that
they are greatly beholden to the church, for every thing
of this kind, wherein they excel themfelves.

And befides this, in proportion as they have become more
acquainted with the church, they have much dropp'd their
great prejudices againft us, and malevolence, and unchari-
tablenefs towards us, and charity, and good neighbourhood
have greatly obtained between us ; fo that, if it was not
for now and then, fuch abufive and uncharitable fcribblings
of a few zealots, full of very injurious mifreprefentations,
we fhould foon coalefce, and come into a friendly, benevolent and chriftian temper, of mutual forbearance towards
one another, and be united in our common weal—I might
add, that in truth the church has been fo far from med-
ling in the various contentions in which they have been almoft continually engaged among themfelves, owing to the
weaknefs of their conftitution, and their republican fepa-
rating and levelling principles, that, to my certain knowledge,

ledge, it hath in many inftances been a great check upon them, and much rather tended to heal and quiet, than ex- afperate them—And as to immoralities, I am fure, the church hath born as faithful a teftimony againft them, in every kind, as any of the diffenters have done ; fo that, if immoralities have increafed, it is not owing to the in- creafe of the church, but to the increafe of mankind here, in proportion to which, from the nature of man, immorali- ties will abound ; I believe however, it may be faid with truth, that in proportion to her numbers, the church can fhew, at leaft as many fober, confcientious chriftians, as the meetings : I know it to be fo, in many places where I am acquainted.

Now, whether it was to give a fpecimen of the Dr's fine talent at ridicule and declamation, or, from a ftudied defign to fright his readers, with an hideous fpectre, that he might create in them all the odium and antipathy he could againft the church of *England*, or, whether it was a little fit of the old diftraction, or, whether after all, the true and principal caufe of his bitternefs againft that found branch of the chriftian church may not ftill be art- fully concealed, I will not take upon me to fay ; but in page 155 you have a moft hideous outcry, about perfecution, hierarchy, tyranny and the like terrible monfters, that made fad work, it feems, an hundred, or an hundred and fifty years ago, from which, however he allows at laft, we have now nothing to fear fince the revolution, from our prefent mild princes, and moderate prelates.—Pray, good fir, what then was the matter with you, when you made this tragical out- cry ? Did you defign to fet a mob upon us ? or what ?

You know very well, that the conftitution of the church is juft the fame now as it was then, and yet fhe abhors per- fecution, and tyranny now, (at leaft) as much as you do : Why fhould fhe then be charged with the doings of tyran- nous courts, or fome perfecuting individuals, fo long ago ? or how can fhe be anfwerable for thofe things, which for almoft thefe hundred years have had no exiftence, nor are ever like to exift again ? or, what fenfe or honefty can there be, in raifing thefe old fpectres, long fince vanifhed and gone, never to revive, meerly to blacken the church,

and

(88)

and render her odious to the present age, while in truth the
church is no more concerned in them, than your party,
who you muft needs know, have perfecuted and tyranniz'd
in their turn, as much, at leaft, as ever the government who
then profefled the church did : You know that perfecution
and toleration are merely political things, in which the
church, as fuch, (being a fpiritual fociety, a kingdom not
of this world,) is in no wife concern'd : The church is the
fame; it is the policy of the flate only, that hath altered,
and I readily agree with you, that in putting an end to perfecution, it hath altered much for the better.

But the good Dr. is ftill terribly diftreffed, about the hierarchy, leaft that fhould obtain here, afcending (as he fays, in his
fine florid way, a-la-mode de independent whig,) *afcending
by various gradations from the dirt to the fkies !* But pray
Dr, be fober a little—We have no pope! There are with
us but three orders; bifhops, presbyters and deacons, according to the model of the pure primitive church, long before the leaft ftep was made towards popery. And we
know that we have ftronger evidence from the *facts* both
of *fcripture* and *antiquity*, for the moft wife, apoftolical,
and confequently divine eftablifhment of thefe three orders,
than you have for infant baptifm, and the firft day fabbath,
of which you are with us fo juftly tenacious.—Your reafoning upon thefe points, and ours for epifcopacy, from the
original facts, is exactly the fame, only we have vaftly the
advantage of you.—If our reafoning for epifcopacy muft
fall, your's on thofe points muft much more fall with it ;
as might be abundantly and inconteftably fhewn, if it was
now before us.— And we do averr, we are certainly as
confcientious in our attachment to our epifcopal form of
church government, as you can be to your presbyterial, or
whatever you call it.—In God's name, then, what reafon
can be given, why we fhould not be allowed to enjoy our
way, as well as you, your's ? We do not envy you, why
fhould you envy and malign us ?——

Pray tell me fir, why we fhould not be allowed in this
country, to be as perfect in our kind, as you, in your's ?
We do not want in the leaft to moleft or oppofe you, in
your way, why then fhould you fo vehemently oppofe
our

our being provided for in our's? You would think it a
terrible thing indeed, (doubtlefs a degree of perfecution,)
to be obliged to go a thoufand leagues for ordination, if it
was your cafe : can you then have no feeling for us whofe
unhappy cafe it is ? In truth fir, we do not aim at any thing
but to live with you in quiet and charitable neighbourhood:
We have not the leaft defire of an epifcopate that fhould
have any thing to do with you, or at all interfere with any
of your proccedings, or, make any alterations among you,
in church or ftate : We only want bifhops, to ordain, and
govern *our own* clergy, to vifit *our* churches, and to inftruct
and confirm *our* laity : And I defire to know, what harm,
fuch a 1 epifcopate could do you ? Nay ; we do not infift
upon a bifhop's refiding in either of your favourite governments : Let him live in one of your heathenifh provinces :
We fhould be content to wait upon him for orders, two or
three hundred miles diftant from you, rather than fail; Why
then fhould you have fuch terrible apprehenfions ?

But the Dr. is moreover in a difmal pannic, left the
church's obtaining in this country, fhould be of ill confequence to it's political affairs.— But why fhould he?
Pray fir be calm—Is not this our country, and the native
country of moft of us, as well as your's ? Can it then be,
that it fhould not be as dear to us, as it is to you ? Have
we not all one common intereft, as to our country's weal,
being embark'd in the fame bottom ? Is it not poffible for us,
each one judging for himfelf, to abound in his own fenfe,
as to matters of religion, and yet live in love, and be united heart and hand, in promoting the publick weal, and our
common interefts, wherein we are all agreed, and equally
concern'd ? I can fee no manner of reafon to the contrary,
or any more danger, left we fhould differ about thefe publick affairs, than if we were all of the fame fentiments in religion : and have we not been as forward in our country's
caufe in the late trying times as any of you ? Difputes will
fometimes arife ; But I cannot fee, why they fhould more
in one cafe, than in the other ? You need not be in the leaft
apprehenfive of the churches being any other wife eftablifhed, than it is already, or that any tefts will obtain in fuch a

M   country

country as this.—Pray fir be eafy, We mean you no harm—
If you would be only as charitable and peaceable toward us,
and among yourfelves, as we are heartily difpofed to be towards you, we might live very quietly and happily together,
and there would be no occafion for another *Columbus*, (as you
cry out) to explore any other *country* for you. We are
neither French, nor Indians, nor Serpents, nor *Dragons* :
Why fo dreadfully afraid of being *confumed by the flames*,
or deluged *in a flood of epifcopacy* ? I realy pity you, that
you fhould fuffer your terrors and paffions fo miferably to run
away with you ! I tell you again, dear fir, we mean you
no harm ; we would only provide for our felves—Pray
do not be fo terribly frighted !— But O my country, dear
New-England, fuffer me to affure you, that you have infinitely more reafon to be afraid of fuch as are no friends to
a co-effential trinity, and the divinity and fatisfaction of
Chrift, (befides other misbeliever's, and unbelievers, of
which there are many,) than of thofe who without cenfuring or aiming to interfere with diffenters, are only defirous
for themfelves to enjoy the church of *England*, in its primitive purity !—

But the Dr. infifts that *Maffachufetts* and *Connecticut*
come not within the Society's limits by the charter : I
anfwer, this cannot be maintained, fince they are not excepted by the charter, unlefs it can be proved that the congregations of the church for which the Society provides in
thofe colonies, would not in the fenfe & words of the charter,
want, or be deftitute of *the adminiftration of God's word
and facraments*, if the Society did not affift them : But
this he does not, nor can he prove. Surely he cannot pretend that King *William*, who introduced the toleration of
diffenters, would leave his loving fubjects of the church un-
tolerated, and under the neceffity of receiving God's word
and facraments contrary to their confciences, or of having
none.— It muft therefore be his meaning to provide, that
his loving fubjects of the church might enjoy God's word
and facraments in thefe colonies, when fuch there are in
competent numbers, for congregations, as well as in other
colonies ;

colonies ; and fo the Society (who muſt be ſuppoſed to be at leaſt as good judges of the meaning of their charter, as Dr. *Mayhew*) have ever underſtood it, and when opportunity offered, have practiſed accordingly, not for the purpoſe of converting diſſenters to the church, but of providing for conſcientious people of the church, and who without this proviſion would have been in danger of as great errors and abſurdities, as thoſe of popery, * and not without danger even of infidelity itſelf, into which I fear many of the diſſenters have been tempted by the abſurd notions of chriſtianity which have been diſſeminated amongſt us.

Now *laſtly,* the great objection is, that the Society neglects the ſouthern colonies, Negroes and Indians,

I anſwer, As to the ſouthern colonies, *Firſt,* The Dr. muſt know, that in *Virginia, Maryland* and *South Carolina,* the church is well provided for by law, ſo that they are out of the queſtion—In *South-Carolina* they are withdrawing their miſſions, as they become vacant.—

Secondly, As to *Georgia,* and the *Bahama* Iſlands, proviſion is made and making for them as faſt as may be, and as their occaſion and application call for. And,

Thirdly, As to *North-Carolina* (over which he drops a pious tear) as far as I can find, ever ſince their application to the Society, they have been providing for them as often as they have been applied to, and as faſt as they could find gentlemen to undertake miſſions, in thoſe tedious and unhealthy climates ; and it appears from the abſtract of 1761, that a great progreſs there is made, and making, and the Society is very much engaged to provide for them, ſo that I imagine thoſe muſt have been diſſenters for whom he is ſo compaſſionate. And,

Fourthly, As to *Penſylvania, New-Jerſies* and *New-York,* I believe no inſtance can be produced, where application

* See Mr. *Beach's* Friendly Expoſtulation, juſt publiſh'd, page 30, 31. &c.

cation has been made to the Society, that has ever been neglected. Indeed, I am sorry to say, there are some few places, where no provision is made for religion, of any sort, that have contracted such an indifference to any at all, (two of which I myself have often urged and engaged my endeavours for them) that they could never be prevail'd upon to embody themselves, to build a church, or take any step towards applying to the Society for their affistance, who would undoubtedly do for them, even to the neglect of *New-England.* Now to such I could wish the Society to send missionaries without being applied to, as they would to *ab origine* heathen, and I truft they will do so, before long, if those people do not apply.

And now, as to *Negroes,* what could the Society do more than it does, and not without some confiderable fuccefs, as appears by the Abftracts—Their missionaries every where inftruct as many as their mafters will fend, and do inftruct and baptize many, and have some communicants—They have feveral catechifts, and Dr. *Bray*'s affociates, feveral fchools (befides that at *Barbadoes*) who conftantly inftruct their children with good fuccefs ; and they have fent one worthy miffionary to *Cape Coaft Caftle,* who laboured there, 'till his health and conftitution were very near ruined.— And,

Laftly, As to the Indians—Many miffionaries have to my knowledge endeavoured to convert them, as they have had opportunity ; and one in particular placed near a confiderable clan of them, endeavoured to reconcile them to chriftianity, 'till fome diffenters fo prejudiced them againft him, that he could do them no Good—And it is well known, that the Society, (always ready to take every opportunity) has fent feveral miffionaries to the *Mohawks,* one after another, from the beginning, and that the Rev. and worthy Dr. *Barclay* was very laborious, with good fuccefs for ten years, inftructed and baptized many, and had a confiderable number of communicants. It is true, he laboured at firft under fome difficulty, for want of an interpreter ; but it was not long before he acquired fo good fkill in their language, as to preach and perform the fervice to their perfect underftanding, and was going

ing on with very good fuccefs, till the laft war, about 1745, threw them into fuch confufion, and the influence of popifh miffionaries, and the wicked infinuations of a certain great man in thofe parts, created fuch a difaffection in them, that his very life was in much danger ; fo that he was obliged to defift.*—However, the Society has ftill a number there not to be defpifed, and much more will foon be done ; one thing they intend in order to it, is, to maintain a number of lads together at *King's College* in *New-York*, to be qualified for miffionaries among them.

Upon the whole, It may be truly faid, what could the Society do more, that it has not done, and all intirely agreeable to the true intention and meaning of their charter. I cannot therefore, imagine but that the candid and ferious, even among the diffenters themfelves, muft be fenfible that Dr. *Mayhew* has moft unjuftly charged the Society, and that his own friends can fcarcely be able to withold a blufh for him, at his indecent, as well as injurious treatment of that venerable body, and of the church, which is a part of the national conftitution ; and alfo, at his mean and unworthy perfonal invectives againft the modeft and very deferving gentleman, who has been the innocent occafion of provoking his riotous pen.—But I muft have done.—I would only add, that the worthy Dr. *Wigglefworth's* letter in the 165th page of Dr. *Mayhew's* book, much deferves the attention of the government both here and in England.—

I am,

Sir, with much Efteem,

Your very hearty Friend and humble Servant,

* So partially and injurioufly, not to fay falfly, does Mr. Smith in his Hiftory of *New York* reprefent this affair.